GUIDELINES FOR EFFECTIVE RESEARCH TO

PUBLICATION: A CONCISE APPROACH

PREFACE

Writing a book on effective research to publication requires an author who has vast experience in research and publishing of research articles. I am fortunately blessed to have had the opportunity to undertake various research works. I have authored 26 scientific research articles that have been published in different journals. I have also designed and taught research methods for both graduate and undergraduate students at California State University, San Bernardino, for over 4 years. I embarked on writing this book as a means of sharing the experiences I have had as a researcher and a full professor. The different research methods classes and each of the manuscripts that I published presented different challenges that are worth sharing. I understand the unique challenges that novice researchers and students who are venturing into scientific research face. I understand the anxiety, disappointment, and stress that come with the rejection of manuscripts and what it means to academic success. I also understand the challenges that the students face balancing research needs and other academic demands. Based on these experiences, I have always had the desire to provide novice researchers and students a simplified book that will enable them to plan their work well and write quality, publishable manuscripts. Therefore, I hope to help novice researchers and students effectively design and execute their research and write quality manuscripts by addressing the technicalities that can result in the rejection of the manuscripts.

I have spent over a year writing this book. The process started with the collection of personal notes and information from my diary. During the first quarter of the year, I went through my research documents—the manuscripts I had successfully published and those that were rejected. I also went through the communications I had with editors and reviewers. In the second quarter of the year, I engaged my peers in conversations about the challenges they faced during their early years of research. I also discussed with them the main areas of focus for writing a quality manuscript that is likely to be accepted by a journal. I also engaged students during the writing process, seeking to further understand the challenges they currently face.

This book aims to guide students and novice researchers on ways of carrying out effective research and writing a publishable manuscript. The first part of the text documents the important feature of quality research. The text provides concise guidelines on how to develop publishable research by describing the key features of the title and the various approaches that should be used in the development of the title. The text also describes the statement of the problem and the features of a well-framed statement of the problem. The text also describes the formulation of an effective research question and the common errors that researchers should avoid. The important aspects of the conceptual and theoretical frameworks are also described, along with the criteria that researchers should use in the development of the conceptual or theoretical framework. The important features of the literature review, methodology, description of the findings, and the abstract are also discussed. Each chapter in the first part of the text concludes with a checklist for the assessment of the individual section.

The second part of the book provides guidelines on the selection and packaging of the manuscript. It describes when and how to identify the appropriate journal. Also, it highlights the steps that should be taken to achieve clarity in writing, enhance the relevance, and avoid plagiarism. I also discuss communication with editors, with an emphasis on how to address the rejection of the manuscript. Finally, the text describes how researchers can ensure effective time management.

I do suggest that researchers who will be using this text as a guide in their research should first consider reading Chapter 12 on time-saving strategies. The chapter enables researchers to effectively plan their work to ensure timely submission of the manuscript. The reader can then read the first eight chapters then proceed to Chapter 9. Chapter 9 enables the readers to select a journal and read the journal's instructions, which provide additional instructions on how to design the methodology, write the results, and provide the discussion.

Acknowledgement

My gratitude goes to God Almighty, whose infinite mercy and grace served as my strength to gather enough resources to complete this book successfully. I am thankful to my loving wife, Frances Chinonso Okpala, BSc, MSc, who carefully read and provided helpful in-depth insights on how to enhance the flow of the information in this book. I am also thankful to my dear children, Vanessa Somtochukwu Okpala (6th grade), Bryan Chiemelie Okpala (3rd grade), Nicole Ifunanya Okpala (1st grade), and Jason Chimaobim Okpala (kindergarten), for understanding the importance of working on this book by giving me the time and space needed to complete this work successfully and comfortably. I also thank my research students and faculty members who have track records of publications, Dr. Monideepa Becerra, full professor in the department of Health Science and Human Ecology, and Dr. Salome Mshigeni, assistant professor in the department of Health Science and Human Ecology, both at California State University, San Bernardino, California, for their encouragement and advice in completing this book.

TABLE OF CONTENTS

PART 1: BASIC GUIDELINES FOR THE DEVELOPMENT OF PUBLISHABLE RESEARCH

CHAPTER 1: SELECTION OF THE TITLE

The title of your research forms the focal point of your paper. It is the first section that the editor and referees check before reading the abstract and the rest of the paper (Bavdekar, 2016). Therefore, it is important to provide an informative and attractive title to catch the attention of the readers. As Huston and Choi (2017 argued), the title should act as a hook that motivates the readers to read the article.

Although the development of the title has been placed as the first chapter in this book, the reader needs to understand that the final title will be developed after completing the research (Bavdekar, 2016). However, the researcher is encouraged to develop a working title at the beginning of the research to act as a guide to ensure focus on the research topic. Thus, instead of fragmenting the development of the title into the different chapters, I consolidated the information under one chapter. This chapter provides the guidelines on the development of an appropriate title that fully communicates the content of the written article. The aspects of the title development that are covered in this chapter include the following:

    i.   Description of the different types of titles

    ii.   Developing a working title

    iii.   Recommendations for writing a good research title

    iv.   Procedures for developing a title

    v.   Checklist for the assessment of an effective title

What Type of Title Fits Your Research?

Although there are as many as 13 types of titles, this book will highlight only three main types (Hartley, 2012). The first type is the declarative title, which is made up of the findings or conclusions of the research. The declarative title is developed after the conclusion of the research (Bavdekar, 2016). The second type is the descriptive title, which is a concise description of the research that does not disclose the findings and conclusions. The description of the research in a descriptive title includes the mention of the main aspects of the research question. A descriptive title allows readers to have complete information about the research and thus enhances the visibility of the manuscript (Habibzadeh & Yadollahie, 2010; Kumar, 2013). The third type of title is the interrogative title, which simply restates the research question.

Developing a Working Title

Although the title is usually developed last, after completion of the research, the working title is important in ensuring the researcher maintains and can regain focus (Bavdekar, 2016). Writing the working title can be a daunting experience for students and novice researchers. One approach that can simplify the process is to adopt a decision cycle process suggested by Saah and Osei (2010). This approach involves the identification of the theme, which involves the description of the subject of the study within the broad program or field of interest. The second step is the development of the topic, using approaches such as tree diagrams and idea maps. The third step is the development of the theories and main terms that will be used within the selected topic and field. A short narrative is then written about the information described above and from the narrative, and a working title is developed (Habibzadeh & Yadollahie, 2010). The approach is considered a cycle because the working narrative will guide the research, and the outcome of the research will guide the development of the final title (Saah & Osei, 2010).

Recommendations for Writing a Good Research Title
First Recommendation: A Good Title Should Communicate Adequate Relevant Information but Still Be Concise

A simple search in search engines such as Google Scholar will reveal that there are several published articles in your area of interest. Therefore, readers are bombarded with several options to choose from and will most often rely on the title when choosing the article to open and read (Bavdekar, 2016). Readers are more likely to choose the most revealing titles because they can easily judge their relevance and suitability. However, because there is a need to balance providing as much relevant information as possible and being concise (Kumar, 2013), researchers should take time to understand and formulate a title that summarizes the entire paper in a few words—usually not more than 15 (Habibzadeh & Yadollahie, 2010).

Second Recommendation: Identify and Employ the Use of Keywords

The use of keywords in the title not only makes it catchy but also increases the chances of the paper being picked up by the literature-scanning services and therefore increases the visibility of your article (Kumar, 2013). Keywords can be located within your research question, in encyclopedias used in background research, or the bibliographies found at the end of the articles and the abstract such as in articles written in APA. Keywords can also be generated using the existing keywords generators, which are free to access (Habibzadeh & Yadollahie, 2010). After choosing the keywords, the next step is to ensure that the placement of the keywords is at the position that makes the terms the focal point of the title. Placing the keywords at the beginning of the title is ideal. Below are examples of good and bad titles based on the placement of the keywords:

Not preferred: Effects of technology adoption on the cost of health care services

Preferred: Technology adoption reduces the cost of health care services

Sometimes the placement of keywords at the beginning of

the title can be cumbersome and can hurt the title's flow. This challenge can be addressed by separating the first part that contains the keyword from the second, which is the explanatory section. The abbreviations such as the colon or a dash can be used to separate the keyword section from the explanatory section. Here is one example of the use of colon in the formulation of titles:

> Power dynamics between nurse and doctors: Identification of steps toward improved health care delivery

Third Recommendation: Choose How to Frame the Title

The title can be framed as a noun phrase, statement, or a question. The noun phrase title is the traditional way of framing the title where a cluster of words and a head noun forms the title. The noun phrase title is usually short and informative and is characterized by the placement of the keyword at the beginning. However, the use of the noun phrase titles is sometimes faced with the possibility of too much generalization, leaving the readers with unanswered questions (Kumar, 2013). Example of a noun phrase title is '*Suppression of cancer progression*'.

Framing the title as a statement is associated with limited

challenges that are associated with the noun phrase approach. Statement titles are characterized by the presence of a subject and a verb. Statement titles tend to give more explicit information about the results of the study (Habibzadeh & Yadollahie, 2010). However, it should be noted that statement titles are only suitable for papers that address a specific question and present a noncomplex answer. This is one example of the statement title: *Technology adoption reduces the cost of health care services.*

In situations where there is no simple answer to the research question, the title can be framed as a question. However, the decision of which framing approach to adopt should be informed by the journal requirements. The author should first read the journal instructions and assess the examples of the articles that have been published in the journal (Habibzadeh & Yadollahie, 2010).

Fourth Recommendation: Be Specific in Noun Phrases

Students and novice researchers should avoid ambiguity when using noun phrases. The use of a string of nouns and adjectives in a title can introduce more than one possible meaning, which can be confusing to the readers. Restricting the noun phrases to a maximum of three words and using a preposition to clarify the meaning of nouns can enhance clarity. The two examples below show a lack of clarity (example 1) and a title with better clarity (example 2).

> **Example 1:** Throat cancer progression suppression

> **Example 2:** Suppression of cancer progression

Procedures for Developing a Title

The final title is written following the completion of the entire manuscript. The first step is to develop a short paragraph that summarizes the manuscript. The second step is to develop working titles, which are made up of sentences with the keywords. The third step is to compress the sentences by eliminating redundancy, enhancing clarity, and increasing the ease of reading. The third step also involves the making of the title catchy by using a provocative statement, a new acronym, or a famous quote (Bavdekar, 2016).

Checklist for the Assessment of an Effective Title

Table 1 provides a checklist for developing the appropriate manuscript title.

Table 1

Checklist for Developing an Appropriate Manuscript Title

Checklist item	Description
Have you adhered to the instructions provided by the journal?	Check the maximum number of words. Check the characters that are allowed, recommended structure, and components.
Is the main theme captured?	The title should explain exactly what the research is all about
Is it clear?	The title should precise, without any form of ambiguity or confusion in interpretation.
Is it of the appropriate length?	The title should be long enough to capture all the required components and should include nothing unnecessary.
Are the keywords captured?	Keywords are required to enhance visibility and discoverability.
Is it attractive and catchy?	Clever use of words captures the reader's attention.
Does it have technical words?	Ensure that the target readers easily understand the title.
Does it have the results of the study?	If incorporated, it should be motivating and unchallengeable.

CHAPTER 2: FORMULATION OF THE PROBLEM

STATEMENT

A poorly written and ineffective problem statement is one of the deficiencies in the proposal and thesis writing that eventually leads to the submission of poor-quality manuscripts. Students and novice researchers need to understand that the problem statement is the heart of the research and therefore warrant diligence when composing it (Flamez, Lenz, Balkin, & Smith, 2017). Apart from the title and the abstract, the problem statement is the first section in a research paper that is given much attention and scrutiny by the assessors and the readers. The problem statement underlines the merits of the research and provides a platform for understanding the research (Flamez et al., 2017).

The problem statement provides the *why* of the research. In research, a phenomenon qualifies to be termed as a problem if it needs a solution and there are different possible options that can provide the needed solution (Wentz, 2013).

In the academic set-up, where there is a limited length of time for students to complete their research (Flamez et al., 2017), students and emerging researchers need to understand that situations (problems) that do not have possible solutions are not worth investing time on. For example, analysis of the definition of time is a problem that exists today, but is it worthy for a physics student to make this his/her research problem? Maybe not. Then, an example of a problem that may need a solution but for which possible solutions seem not to exist is the problem of death. Therefore, students who analyze how people can achieve immortality will not make any sense, at least in our current understanding of reality.

It is, therefore, important for students to understand how to frame a problem statement that leads to research questions that are measurable and can be tested using the appropriate scientific approach. This section provides guidelines on how to write an effective problem statement and the pitfalls that one should avoid when writing the section. The aspects of the problem of the statement that are addressed in this chapter include the following:

    i.   Definition of the term

    ii.   Importance of the problem statement

    iii.   Features of a well-framed problem statement

    iv.   Materials needed to formulate a problem statement

    v.   Checklist for the assessment of an effective problem statement

What Is a Problem Statement?

As already hinted in the introduction to this section, the term *problem statement*, as used in research, refers to the existing situation that needs to be assessed to identify the appropriate solution (Wentz, 2013). The problem statement is basically one sentence that specifically identifies the issues that needs to be addressed (Flamez et al., 2017). However, for the problem statement to be complete, the issue stated in that one sentence needs to be qualified using several sentences and sometimes paragraphs (Wentz, 2013).

Why Is the Problem Statement Important?

A well-framed problem statement is vital because it provides the importance of the research and helps hook the reader into the research (Dine, McGaghie, Bordage, & Shea, 2015). Incorporating a well-written problem statement into your work helps readers identify the context of your research without needing to read the entire literature review and the arguments you make in the background section (Flamez et al., 2017). The readers also get an opportunity to identify the questions that your research seeks to address. A well-framed problem statement also directs the reader on how the study will add to the literature. Finally, the problem statement also provides a platform for introducing the research questions, hypotheses, and/or assumptions (Flamez et al., 2017).

What Are the Features of a Well-Framed Problem Statement?

There are three main features of a well-written problem statement. Each of the features is described below.

The Problem

As is evident from the name and its definition, students need to indicate the unique problem/issue/ situation that is being assessed. Usually, the problem is stated in the opening sentence of the first paragraph.

Context

The term *context* is used to refer to the background or the literature that provides persuasive arguments on the importance of the stated problem. Contextualizing the problem and situating it within the existing literature in the field of study is important in establishing how the solutions to the stated problem will add new knowledge to the existing literature. The context also identifies the population of interest. The problem statement is also made up of sentences that identify where the problem exists (the setting; Dine et al., 2015).

Purpose/Research Questions/Statement of the Objectives

The problem statement also needs to incorporate the sentences that highlight the purpose of research. A good problem statement also provides the scope of the study.

Methods/Research Approach

A well-written problem statement needs to identify the approach that will be used to address the stated problem. The elements of the methodology that should be mentioned in the problem statement include the variables (for quantitative studies) and the data sources. The approach/methods in the problem statement are often stated as a claim, which allows room for further development as the research progresses (Flamez et al., 2017).

What Material Is Needed to Formulate a Problem Statement?

For researchers to formulate a well-written problem statement, they need to have a good grasp of the relevant literature and the existing gap in the literature (Wentz, 2013). However, there is a need to identify the research question before immersing yourself into the literature review. Thus, before writing the problem statement, students are encouraged to invest time in extensive research into the existing knowledge regarding the topic of interest (Flamez et al., 2017). Some of the areas of the literature review that the students should pay keen attention when developing the problem statement include results from the previous researchers that were not fully explored and that relate to the identified research question. Personal experiences, especially when conducting qualitative research, also provide material used in formulating the problem statement.

Checklist for the Assessment of an Effective Problem Statement

Table 2 provides a checklist for the evaluation of the appropriate statement of the problem.

Table 2

Checklist for the Evaluation of the Appropriate Statement of the

Problem

Item	Description
Is the problem identified?	This should be in the first sentence.
Is the problem evidence-based?	The evidence should be supported by recent literature.
Is the methodological approach identified?	The research design and paradigm needed to address the problem should be highlighted.
Is the context and population of interest described?	The population affected by the problem should be mentioned along with the geographic area.
Is the gap in literature identified appropriately?	The gap in the literature should be used to explain the importance of the problem and why it needs to be addressed.

CHAPTER 3: FORMULATION OF THE RESEARCH QUESTION

An initial important step in the development of a high-quality manuscript that meets the journals' requirements, addresses an area of importance to the target readership, and adds value to the existing literature is the identification of a research question. The research question needs to be clear and well articulated so there is no doubt in the mind of the reader about what the researcher wants to know. A researcher needs to ask what specific challenges the work seeks to address or what condition the work seeks to improve on. Because the formulated research question defines the relevance of the study to the journal and the field of interest, researchers need to be sufficiently equipped with skills on how to prepare relevant, interesting, and researchable research questions.

This section seeks to provide novice researchers and students with tools needed to formulate an effective research question. The aspects of the research question formulation that are addressed in this include the following:

i. Types of research questions

ii. When to develop the research question

iii.   What to consider when developing a research question

iv.   Common errors in the formulation of the research question

v.   Research question and the research design

vi.   Checklist for the assessment of an effective research question

Types of Research Questions

The research question can be interrogative or declarative. The declarative research question is expressed as a statement that indicates the purpose of the study. The interrogative research question is framed as a question that identifies a gap in knowledge in the area of interest.

When to Develop the Research Question

The entire research is aimed at addressing the research question. Therefore, it is advisable to develop the research question before developing other sections. Because the research question determines the relevant literature to be reviewed, it needs to be formulated before the literature review (Churchill & Sanders, 2007). Researchers also need to develop the research question first, then identify the research design required to answer the research question. However, the development of the research question is an iterative process that might require the student to return and reevaluate the research question as the research progresses. The iterative process ensures the development of a relevant, specific, and answerable research question.

What to Consider When Developing a Research Question

The questions that students need to ask themselves when formulating a research question are discussed in this section.

What Is the Motivation for the Research?

The researcher needs to have a good understanding of what inspires him or her to carry out the research. Is it personal/professional experiences? Academic demands?

What Do I Want to Know? What Is Known Already?

Determining what you know about the topic of interest is important in framing the research question. The researcher needs to examine the relevant literature critically to identify gaps (Churchill & Sanders, 2007). The gaps are then framed as the absence of the solution(s) you want to suggest. What this means is that for every question you want to pose, you need to apply circular reasoning. You should already have assumptions regarding the key aspects of the research question. For example, consider this sample research question: *What is the impact of technological adoption in the cost of health care services?* There are two assumptions in this research question:

1. There is technological adoption in the health care

2. Technological adoption can influence the cost of health care services

The assumptions embedded in the research question should be evidence-based.

Determining what others have done in the area of interest helps prevent attempts to reinvent the wheel, which is common among enthusiastic novice researchers. Reviewing what others have done can make the work of researchers less tedious and more valuable because it enables one to narrow the research question to the existing gaps in literature (Churchill & Sanders, 2007). Knowing what has been done also ensures that the question that is posed maximizes the participants' time and the researcher's resources by engaging in worthwhile research.

Do You Have the Time?

Asking whether you have sufficient time and resources requires the researcher to examine the time and the resources that will be required to collect, manage, and analyze the data to address the question adequately.

Do You Have the Required Expertise?

The research question determines the research design, data collection approach, and the type of analysis to be undertaken. It is therefore advisable for researchers to choose research questions they have the intellectual and technical capacity to answer.

Is It Possible to Obtain the Data?

Being able to collect the required data to answer the question is an important consideration. Researchers should be cautious not to pose questions that will require them to collect data on controversial or sensitive behavior. Researchers also need to be cautious when posing questions that might require them to collect data from participants who lack the incentive to participate or do not trust the research process or the researcher. Researchers also need to avoid posing questions that require them to collect data from the inaccessible participants (Churchill & Sanders, 2007). It is also advisable to avoid posing questions that require the collection of classified data or where ethical issues are associated with the data collection process.

Where Should Research Questions Be Placed?

The research question should be mentioned in the abstract and introduction, and it is sometimes identified in the title, which helps the readers to discern the potential relevance of the manuscript to their area of interest.

Common Errors in the Formulation of the Research Question

Various errors prevent students and novice researchers from formulating an effective research question. Some of the common errors, as provided in Table 3, include those discussed in this section.

Lack of Specificity

One commonly committed error is posing the research

question in broad terms so that the researcher indicates the topic instead of the specific problem (Churchill & Sanders, 2007). In the example provided in Table 3, it is not obvious what is going to be explored: the nature of power dynamics (how power is shared in health care teams), the effect of power dynamics on a team's performance of the team, or how the members of health care teams view power dynamics. The corrected research question helps specify the research problem and directs the readers and the study toward a specific issue (factors influencing power dynamics) within the broad topic of power dynamics in health care teams.

Lack of Sense

Some research questions do not add any value to existing knowledge, and it therefore makes no sense investigating them.

Being Trivial

Stating a trivial research question is another problem that is common among students. Based on the third example (Problem 3) of ineffective research question provided in Table 3, the researchers are restricted to a yes or no answer, which is too simple and provides insufficient information about the research phenomenon.

Table 3

Common Problems When Developing an Effective Research

Question

	Ineffective Research Question	Problems	Corrected Research Question
Problem 1	Power dynamics in health care teams	Identification of the topic (area), not the research problem	What factors influence power dynamics in inter-professional health care teams?
Problem 2	Does healthy eating improve overall health?	The research problem is not of value or does not make sense	How does food portion affect the influence of healthy eating On overall health?
Problem 3	Are ethicist consultants' good communicators?	The research problem is trivial or too simple	What communication tools do ethicist consultants use? What factors affect communication among ethicist consultants? How does communication among ethicist consultants affect the client's satisfaction?

Research Question and the Research Design

The research question for the qualitative and quantitative research design varies. Thus, the researcher needs to ensure that there is congruence between the research question and the research design (Churchill & Sanders, 2007). When deciding the research design that best addresses the research question, one should ask these questions: What kind of data is needed to answer the research question? Who are the participants? How will the data be collected? How will the data be analyzed?

Framing Research Questions for Qualitative Studies

For qualitative designs, interrogative research questions are mainly used where the questions take the form of "What is this?" Or "What is happening here?" These designs are more concerned with the process rather than the outcome (Agee, 2009). When framing the qualitative research question, students need to understand the phenomenon, issue, or event they want to know more about. They should then choose the keywords or phrases that will help them focus on their phenomenon. The keywords that can be used include construct, interpret, understand, negotiate, perceive, and explore (Churchill & Sanders, 2007). When designing the research question for qualitative research, it is also important to identify the actors (the target population), the setting, and the phenomenon of interest. Look at the following example of a qualitative research question: *How do students in institutions of higher learning perceive racial discrimination?* In this example, students represent the people (actors), an institution of higher learning is the setting, and racial discrimination is the phenomenon. The term *'perceive'* is used as the keyword (Agee, 2009).

Framing Research Questions for Quantitative Studies

A quantitative research question restates the topic of interest in operational terms to allow the gathering of empirical data used to test an already-stated hypothesis. For quantitative research questions, students need to have a good understanding of various concepts, such as a unit of analysis, variable, and attributes (Churchill & Sanders, 2007). The *unit of analysis* refers to objects or events that are being counted or measured. In a survey, people represent the unit of analysis. A *variable* is a concept that measurably describes a phenomenon. The variable can either be dependent (dv), a concept that is acted upon by another variable, independent (iv), one that acts upon the other variable(s), or mediating, one that influences the relationship between the dependent and independent variables. *Attributes* are the categories within variables, such as male and female attributes for the variable gender.

The hypothesis is logically linked to the research question and states the relationship between variables. With a quantitative research question, the hypothesis should be tested by gathering empirical data, which requires the use of measurable variables. The description of how the hypothesis influences the development of the research question is described in Table 4.

Table 4

Framing a Quantitative Research Question Guided by the Hypothesis

	Step 1	Hypothesis Formulation			Step 5
		Step 2	Step 3	Step 4	Feedback on the research question
Description	Initial research question: Is Variable 1 related to Variable 2	Identification of iv	Identification of the direction of the relationship	Phrasing the hypothesis to answer the research question and making a testable prediction	Reformulation of the research question
Example	Is the cost of health care related to the adoption of technology?	Adoption of technology is the iv and therefore, comes first	Increased adoption of technology is likely to decrease the cost of health care.	The greater the adoption of technology, the higher the reduction in the cost of health care.	Are health care institutions with increased adoption of technology likely to charge less for health care services?

A summary of the possible research questions and the appropriate research designs are provided in Table 5.

Table 5

Selected Research Questions and Associated Research Designs

Research Question	Research Design
Seeks people's responses to the already-stated questions	Survey
Seeks people's account of their experiences when the researcher is not sure what is important	Open-ended interview
Seeks people's real-time account and detailed description of events as they occurred	Diary study
Seeks participants' behavior in their natural setting	Observation

Checklist for the Assessment of an Effective Research Question

Table 6 provides a checklist for a good research question.

Table 6

Checklist for a Good Research Question

Item	Description
Feasible	Accessible and adequate sample size; sufficient expertise to address it; sufficient time and resources; manageable in scope
Interesting	The question that the researcher is sincerely interested and/or invested in
Novel	Builds on previous research, but also offers something new
Ethical	Takes ethical issues into consideration; can be approved by the institutional review board
Relevant	Grounded in a theoretical framework; can suggest directions for future research; addresses some real problem in the world directly or indirectly

CHAPTER 4: DEVELOPING THE CONCEPTUAL FRAMEWORK/ THEORETICAL FRAMEWORK

The terms *theoretical framework* and *conceptual framework* are some of the most confusing to students carrying out research. A good grasp of the two terms is important because they are vital in writing quality and credible manuscripts (McKercher, Law, Weber, Song, & Hsu, 2007). Most students and faculty members often apply the two terms incorrectly in their research, which weakens their findings. Without a good application of a theoretical or conceptual framework in research, the readers experience difficulties in ascertaining the academic position of such papers and the motivation for the developed hypotheses and research questions.

This chapter, therefore, seeks to enhance the understanding of theoretical framework or conceptual frameworks among researchers. The aspects of the theoretical framework and conceptual framework that will be addressed in this chapter include the following:

- Differences between theoretical framework and conceptual framework

- Importance of theoretical framework and conceptual

framework in research

- Selection of an appropriate theoretical framework

- Construction of an appropriate conceptual framework

- Steps to follow when developing the conceptual framework

- Checklist for the assessment of an effective conceptual and theoretical framework

Differences between Theoretical Framework and Conceptual Framework

Various researchers describe the two terms using different terminologies, but all definitions have a common theme. The theoretical framework has been defined as a map or a blueprint that guides the research process (Fulton & Krainovich-Miller, 2010). The term is also defined as a set of theoretical principles, constructs, concepts, and tenets of a theory that guide the research process (Adom et al., 2016; Grant & Osanloo, 2014). The conceptual framework, on the other hand, is defined as the structure that describes the progression of the phenomenon being studied (Adom et al., 2016). The term is also a description of how the researchers envision the relationship between the variables being studied. The conceptual framework is therefore defined as the logical description of the relationship between the main concepts of a study (Grant & Osanloo, 2014). Both the theoretical and conceptual frameworks can be presented using graphical representation or in a narrative form (Adom et al., 2016).

Unlike the theoretical framework, the conceptual framework focuses on specific or narrower ideas that are specific to the research question and the purpose and significance of the study. The theoretical framework, on the other hand, positions the study within a broader worldview. The theories that make up the theoretical framework are not the creation of the authors but concepts that have been tested and validated by other scholars. However, the researcher creates the conceptual framework using specific variables that are selected from the study's research questions. The theoretical framework also differs from the conceptual framework in that the latter focuses on testing theories while the former aims at developing theories regarding the phenomenon of interest (Adom et al., 2016).

What Is the Importance of Theoretical and Conceptual Framework in Research?

Table 7 provides a summary of the importance of the theoretical framework and conceptual framework. The described benefits show that theoretical and conceptual frameworks are important components of research. Therefore, students who aim to produce a quality, publishable research paper need to consider incorporating theoretical and/or conceptual frameworks in their research.

Table 7

Importance of Theoretical Framework and Conceptual

Framework in Research

Theoretical Framework	Conceptual Framework
The theoretical framework provides the researcher's philosophical, epistemological, and methodological definition of the study (Grant & Osanloo, 2014).	The conceptual framework provides a platform upon which the researcher can develop his/her worldview on the phenomenon of interest (Adom et al., 2016).
It contextualizes the study within the existing literature and therefore positions it in a scholarly and academic fashion (Adom et al., 2016).	It provides the reasons why the research is worth carrying out (Akintoye, 2015).
It is the focus of the research, and its links to the research question guide the selection of the research design and data analysis approach.	It describes the researcher's assumptions regarding the relationship between the various aspects of the research phenomenon (Evans, 2007).
It determines the type of data to be collected, and it allows for effective generalization of the study findings.	It provides the conceptual grounding of the research approach (Adom et al., 2016).
It opens up the researcher's worldview of the phenomenon of interest and provides a basis upon which the researchers can challenge their perspective against the competing theories (Akintoye, 2015).	It is used as an alternative when the existing theories are insufficient to provide the logical research structure (Akintoye, 2015)

Selection of an Appropriate Theoretical Framework

According to Grant and Osanloo (2014), there is not a perfect theory for a given study. How then does one choose a given theory and leave out the others? The selection of a suitable theoretical framework is based on the researcher's in-depth understanding of the research problem, purpose, and significance and the research question (Adom et al., 2016; Simon & Goes, 2011). A suitable theoretical framework is also that which emphasizes the purpose and importance of the research (Grant & Osanloo, 2014). Therefore, when choosing the theoretical framework, researchers need to ensure that the chosen theories are in agreement with the research question and the study purpose (LoBiondo-Wood & Haber, 2014). Thus, the discussion of the study findings must gravitate toward the corroboration, expansion, modification or the critique of the chosen theoretical framework (Adom et al., 2016). The questions that the researchers should ask themselves when selecting the theoretical framework include the following:

- Is there congruency between the selected theory and the methodology plan for the study?

- Are the theoretical constructs within the selected

theory sufficient to guide the study?

- Is there congruency between the selected theory's concepts and the objectives of the study?

- Is there congruency between the selected theory and the problem, purpose, and importance of the study?

- Is the selected theory relevant to the discipline?

- Is there agreement between the selected theory and the research questions?

- Does the selected theoretical framework give relevance to the literature review?

- Is there agreement between the selected theory and the data analysis plan?

- Does the selected theoretical framework inform the discussion, conclusion, and recommendations of the study?

Construction of an Appropriate Conceptual Framework

It is the responsibility of the researchers to construct the conceptual framework (Adom et al., 2016; Polit & Tatano, 2004). The conceptual framework is constructed using diagrams that define the variables and show how they relate to each other.

Although researchers can adopt the existing frameworks, researchers need to modify such frameworks to fit the specific research and the research question. The developed conceptual framework also needs to agree with the research context (Latham, 2017). Then, after developing the graphical representation of the relationship between the different variables, researchers need to describe the diagram in the text (Fisher, 2007). The following are examples of conceptual frameworks adopted from published articles. It is evident from the examples that the conceptual framework needs to agree with the study title, and the objective and all hypotheses emerge from the conceptual framework.

Example 1: Saleem (2015)

Title: The impact of leadership styles on job satisfaction and the mediating role of perceived organizational politics

Objectives: To investigate the impact of leadership styles on job satisfaction and to see if perceived organizational politics has a mediating role or not.

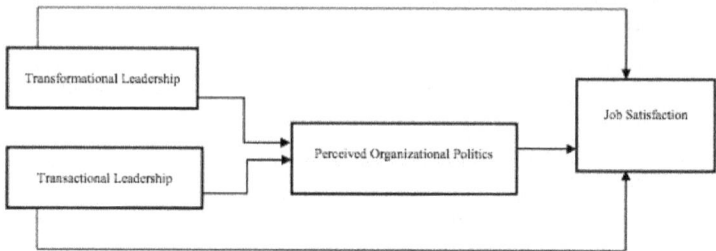

Figure 1. The conceptual framework developed by Saleem (2015)

Study hypothesis:

H1: There is a relationship between transformational leadership and job satisfaction

H2: There is a relationship between transactional leadership and job satisfaction

H3: There is a relationship between transformational leadership and perceived organizational politics

H4: There is a relationship between transactional leadership and perceived organizational politics

H5: There is a relationship between perceived organizational politics and job satisfaction

H6: Perceived organizational politics is a mediator between transformational leadership and job satisfaction

H7: Perceived organizational politics is a mediator between transactional leadership and job satisfaction.

Example 2: Rezvani et al. (2016)

Title: Manager emotional intelligence and project success: The mediating role of job satisfaction and trust

Objectives: To understand how project managers' emotional intelligence (EI) contributes to project success and to explore potential mechanisms by which an emotionally intelligent project manager may contribute to project success factors

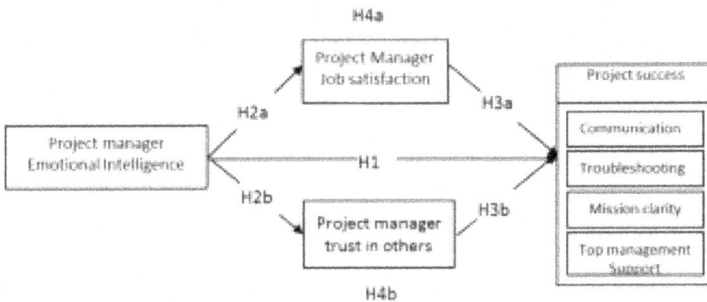

Figure 2. The conceptual framework developed by Rezvani et al. (2016)

Study hypotheses:

> H1: Project managers' EI is positively related to project success.

> H2: Project managers' EI is positively related to (a) their job satisfaction and (b) their trust in others.

> H3: There is a positive relationship between project

managers' trust in others and project success.

H4: Project managers' job satisfaction is positively related to project success.

H5: Project managers' attitudes, namely (a) job satisfaction and (b) trust, mediate the relationship between project managers' EI and project success.

Steps to Follow When Developing the Conceptual Framework

The following steps need to be followed when constructing a conceptual framework:

1. Examine and understand the research title and research problem.

2. Determine the key variables in your research.

3. Review related literature to learn how to build assumptions regarding identified variables.

4. List the constructs and variables.

5. Document the assumptions regarding the relationship between the constructs and variables using graphical representation.

Checklist for the Assessment of an Effective Conceptual and

Theoretical Framework

Table 8 provides a checklist for evaluating the conceptual and theoretical framework.

Table 8

Checklist for Evaluating the Conceptual Framework and the

Theoretical Framework

Theoretical Framework	Conceptual Framework
Does it provide the philosophical, epistemological, and methodological definition of the study?	Does it provide the graphical representation of the relationship between the different aspects of the research phenomenon and research question?
Does it contextualize the study within the existing literature?	Is it grounded in the relevant literature?
Does it connect the research question to the research design and data analysis?	Does it describe the researcher's assumptions regarding the relationship between variables?
Does it identify the type of data to be collected?	Does it provide details regarding the research approach?

CHAPTER 5: GUIDELINES FOR CARRYING OUT

A FOCUSED LITERATURE REVIEW

A literature review is a multistage undertaking that involves scanning the information, documenting the obtained information, synthesizing and structuring the information, and writing a critical review of the obtained evidence. The literature review provides the background for the entire research topic and is important in discovering what has already been written about a topic. It also situates the identified research focus within the context of the relevant wider academic community, and a well-written literature review facilitates the understanding of the existing relationship between the contributions of the various authors to the research area, identifies contradictions, and, if possible, suggests resolutions to these contradictions (McKercher et al., 2007). Importantly, the literature review helps determine the gaps or unanswered questions.

Students face various challenges when writing the literature review. These are some of the challenges faced when writing the literature review:

- Deciding on a topic for the literature search

- Identifying the relevant sources of information

- Extracting data from the selected studies

- Understanding how to link the information together
  and develop a critical analysis of the obtained
  information

Writing a focused literature review is central to an effective research process. This section provides a stepwise approach to writing a literature review to ensure that the writing process is focused and associated with limited challenges.

Steps in Writing a Focused Literature Review

Developing a focused literature review is a systematic process that involves various steps. The steps provided below are based on my experiences, in-depth research, and years of sharing experiences with seasoned writers. Although the steps are presented as a sequential process, it should be noted that some of the steps can be undertaken concurrently. The five steps for conducting an effective literature review are as follows:

1. Developing a mind map

2. Material search and extracting of relevant data

3. Piecing the ideas together

4. Developing a critical analysis

Developing a Mind Map

Before writing the literature review section, one needs to develop a mind map (Kalyanasundaram et al., 2017). Mind mapping the literature can only be carried out once a research question has been developed (Hart, 2018). Therefore, the first step in the development of the mind map involves the question *why*, which is answered by a clear and complete statement of your research question (Kalyanasundaram et al., 2017).

This is one example of a clear and complete research question: What is the impact of technological adoption on the cost of health care services? (adapted from Okpala, 2018).

The second step is identifying the key terms, concepts, and phrases from the identified research question. This step involves the underlining of the terms that form the basis of the research question. The key terms (T1, T2, and T3) that can be identified from the example of research question provided above are shown in Figure 3 below:

Figure 3: identification of the key terms within research questions for the development of the mind map

The third step involves identifying the questions that emanate from the terms that were identified in step two and the questions that flow from the research question as a whole (Kalyanasundaram et al., 2017). During this step, it is also important to develop generic questions that form the focus of the literature review (Hart, 2018). Some of the generic questions include the motivations for research, such as the significance of the area of study, deficiencies in existing knowledge, sources of new ideas, and questions regarding the theory (Hart, 2018). The fourth step in the development of the mind map is the development of follow-up questions and links to the questions in step three. An example of the mind map that is relevant to the example research question is provided in Figure 4.

How do they compare with competing theories?

How do these theories inform my methodological approach?

Do the cost associated with conventional approaches differ from the technology based approaches?

How relevant are these theories?

What theories help to understand the relationship between technological adoption and cost of health services ?

Why is the cost important?

What is the impact of technological adoption on the cost of healthcare services?

What do I know about the impact?

Which technologies I am talking about?

What are the existing gaps in the understand of impact of tech on cost?

Do they all have the same impact on cost?

Why is it important to address the gaps?

How can I address the gaps?

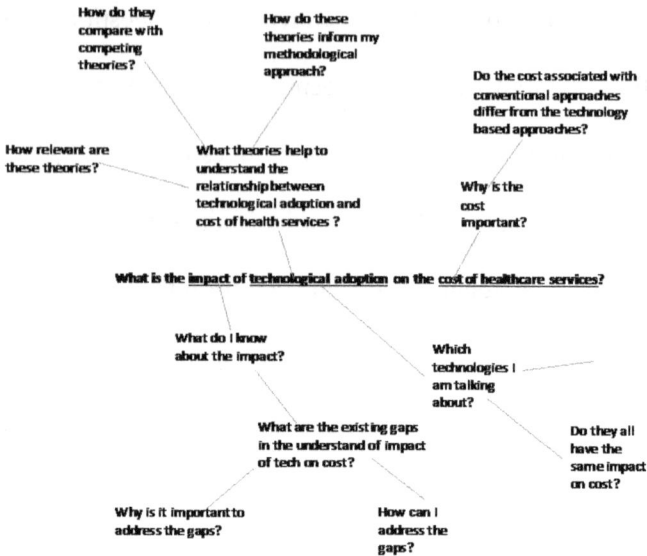

Figure 4. An example of mind mapping

The development of the mind map is a continuous process that can stretch into the actual writing process (Kalyanasundaram et al., 2017). Researchers should develop new questions and add to the map as they get new ideas from reading or engaging in discussion on various topics related to the research study (Hart, 2018). The mind map helps students address the challenges that were listed in the introduction, such as the identification of the relevant information and the topical areas that should be addressed by the literature review.

Material Search and Extracting Relevant Data

Sources of relevant material include material that is used in writing of the literature. These sources can be found using electronic databases, information libraries, and within the bibliographies of other resources.

Electronic Sources

Searching electronic sources is probably the quickest way to access a lot of material. Electronic resources are material in digital format that is accessible electronically (Randolph, 2009). Examples of electronic resources are electronic journals (e-journal), electronic books (e-book) online databases in varied digital formats, Adobe Acrobat documents (.pdf), web pages (.htm, .html, .asp etc.) and more.

Identifying quality sources. Web material is volatile; it changes frequently, becomes outdated, or is deleted. Because much web material does not have stringent quality control, students are faced with the challenge of determining the quality and relevance of the collected material (Randolph, 2009). This book recommends the use of the checklist in Table 9 in assessing the quality of the electronic material.

Table 9

Checklist for Assessing the Quality of Electronic Sources

Item	Questions to Ask
Authority	Who is the author? Is there a way of verifying the legitimacy of the author? Is the writer qualified? Is the source known to be reliable?
Accuracy	Is it possible to verify the factual information? Can one opinion be verified against another? Is the material free of grammatical and spelling errors?
Objectivity	Is the material free of conflict of interest or bias? Does the material have any link to a company/organization or another web page? Is there any advertising? Is the statistical evidence credible? Is the language free from any partiality?
Currency	Is the chosen material up to date? Are the findings based on the most recent data? When was the material published? Are there more recent publications on the same topic?
Coverage	Is the topic of interest well covered by the material with arguments that are well supported? Is the material within the context of your research? Does the material add new information or update on the recent sources?

Identifying appropriate search terms/keywords. The research question is the primary source of the keywords for your search (Cronin, Ryan, & Coughlan, 2008). Unlike a topic, which gives broad key terms that may not be relevant to the study, the research question provides specific key terms (Randolph, 2009). The first step in identifying the key terms from the research question is choosing the words from within your question that are the most important to your search. Figure 5 shows the key terms (T1, T2, T3, T4, and T5) that have been selected from the research question.

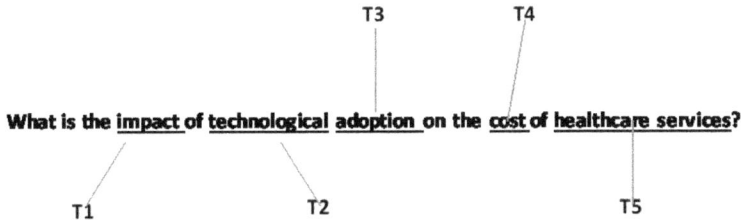

T3   T4

What is the impact of technological adoption on the cost of healthcare services?

T1   T2   T5

Figure 5: Identification of key terms from research question

The second step is using the identified key terms to search the selected electronic database. Then, from the obtained articles, identify alternative search words that are used and identify their synonyms. Use the identified alternative terms to carry out a further search in the selected electronic database.

Information Libraries

Information such as the policy documents, standards, archive material, videos, and audio recordings, which may not be available electronically, can be located in the brick-and-mortar library. Searching of journals can also be carried out in the library as the researcher goes through the most important journals for the selected research topic (Cronin et al., 2008; Randolph, 2009).

Material from the Bibliographies

After identifying the relevant research material and articles, additional articles can be obtained from the bibliographies of the relevant studies (Cronin et al., 2008).

Determining the quality of the retrieved articles. After finding articles based on the research question, it is important to appraise the quality of those articles. The critical appraisal of the selected material aims at answering four main questions (Table 10). The more "no" responses, the lower the quality of the article.

Table 10

Summary of the Critical Appraisal Tool

Question	YES	NO
Does this study address a clearly focused question?		
Did the study use valid methods to address this question?		
Are the valid results of this study important?		
Are these valid, important results applicable to my study population?		

Various useful tools exist that help in answering the four questions in Table 10. The available Critical Appraisal Worksheets vary based on the nature of the selected article. The links to the various Critical Appraisal Worksheets are provided in Appendix I.

Extraction of Data

Data are extracted from selected studies and other official documents. Thus, it is important for researchers to develop inclusion and exclusion criteria that are appropriate for their study. See Cochrane (2019) for further details on the development of appropriate selection criteria. The data collection process is carried out using the data collection sheet. The data collection sheets vary based on the nature of the study (Randolph, 2009). However, the data collection sheet should contain at least the following prompts:

Authorship/identity: The name of the author, title of the study, date of publishing, and country of origin (where the data were collected)

Objectives and methodology: Participants, recruitment procedure, data collection approach, data analysis, limitations, and strengths of the study

Results: The relevant findings to the research question, baseline findings, completeness of the findings, and missing participants

Discussion: Key conclusions, emerging gaps, and comparison with other studies

It is best practice for researchers to tailor the data collection sheets to fit their needs. It is also important for researchers to pilot their data collection tools to ensure effectiveness. The examples of the data collection sheets provided in Table 11 indicate the variations that exist across different studies.

Table 11

Example of a Data Collection Sheet

Source	Data Collection Sheet Content
Brizay et al. (2015)	1. Article: Author, title. 2. Year of publication 3; Publication type; 4. Term used (PAR, AR, CBR, CBPR, or other). 5. Original definition of term. 6. Cited definition of term, including source. 7. Period of data collection; 8. Country (where study took place). 9. Objective of article/study. 10. Study type. 11. Study methodology. 12. Study target group.13. Who was the community partner? 14. Community advisory board. 15. Role of community partner.16. Who took initiative for the research? 17. Results dissemination to community. 18. Institutional Review Board (IRB) approval. 19. Which institution gave IRB approval? 20. Ethical approval by community. 21. Which capacity-building activities took place? 22. What was the added value of the community involvement? 23. What were the negative aspects/limitations of community involvement? 24. Did the community involvement lead to changes in the community? 25. Funding agency. 26. Other partners involved
Staggers and Blaz (2013)	1. Author, year of publication, country. 2. Target group, number of participants. 3. Method of CTG training. 4. Other training components. 5. Method of evaluation. 6. Kirkpatrick level. 7. Results

Piecing the Ideas Together

One of the mistakes students make when putting together the information collected from the various sources is to discuss each of the sources separately. While this might be a simple approach, the outcome does not allow for critical analysis of the various pieces of evidence and the identification of the areas of convergence and/or divergence (Hart, 2018; Randolph, 2009). Best practice, therefore, requires the researchers to discuss more than one source in every paragraph. Three main approaches can be used to piece the collected ideas together. Each of the approaches is discussed below.

Theme Approach

This is the most common way to organize literature reviews. Information from the different sources is extracted and categorized into themes. The different studies are then compared to how they address (i.e., support/contradict) the identified theme. The thematic approach is commonly used when explaining key themes or issues relevant to the topic (Cronin et al., 2008).

Methodology Approach

The methodology approach is commonly used when discussing interdisciplinary approaches to a topic or when discussing a number of studies with a different approach.

Chronological Approach

The chronological approach is commonly used for topics that have been discussed for a long time and have changed over their history. The content is organized based on how the topic has changed over time. The major periods of change are highlighted and defined adequately.

Broad to Specific Guideline

When using any of the three approaches highlighted above to organize the information, it is best practice to start with the broad picture and narrow down to a specific idea (Figure 6). It is important to note that the broad to specific approach is also applicable within the subsections of the literature review and in the individual paragraphs. Each paragraph needs to have a topic sentence, which provides the general and broad picture (Randolph, 2009). The broad to specific approach is suitable when introducing the background and related facets of the research topic that have a less direct relationship to the topic but are important in tying the many related, broader articles together (Hart, 2018). However, when starting with the broader problem area, the students should avoid making global statements that may fail to identify with the research area or the evidence presented.

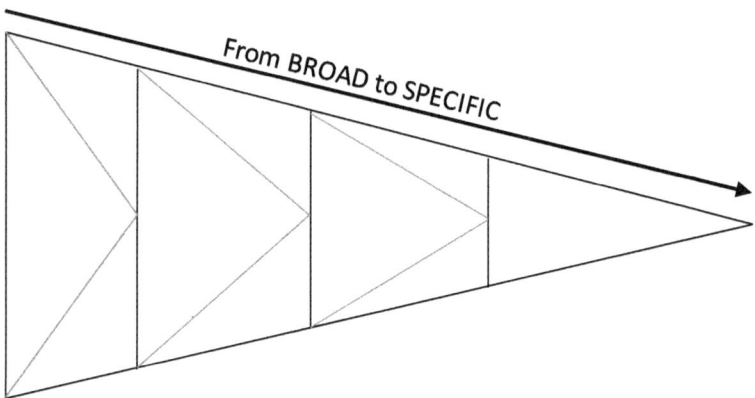

Figure 6. Representation of the broad to specific guideline

The small triangles within the large triangle indicate the need to adopt the guideline within the subsections of the literature review.

Figure 7 below shows the broad to specific approach. In this example, the author is focusing on power dynamics in health care teams (submitted for publishing). He starts by providing the bigger picture through the discussion of the importance of effective health care in the provision of quality health care, which then allows him to introduce the importance of the balance of power. The author then introduces the role of health care leaders in ensuring the balance of power in health care teams to achieve effective delivery of service, which leads to the gap that the study sought to address: developing a conclusive and in-depth understanding of the strategies that managers can use to address power dynamics in health care teams (Figure 7).

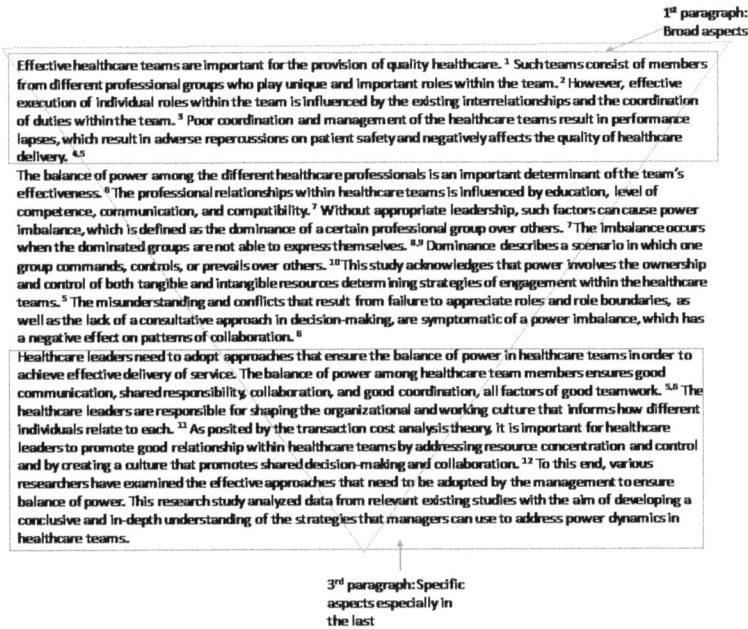

1ˢᵗ paragraph: Broad aspects

Effective healthcare teams are important for the provision of quality healthcare. [1] Such teams consist of members from different professional groups who play unique and important roles within the team. [2] However, effective execution of individual roles within the team is influenced by the existing interrelationships and the coordination of duties within the team. [3] Poor coordination and management of the healthcare teams result in performance lapses, which result in adverse repercussions on patient safety and negatively affects the quality of healthcare delivery. [4,5]

The balance of power among the different healthcare professionals is an important determinant of the team's effectiveness. [6] The professional relationships within healthcare teams is influenced by education, level of competence, communication, and compatibility. [7] Without appropriate leadership, such factors can cause power imbalance, which is defined as the dominance of a certain professional group over others. [7] The imbalance occurs when the dominated groups are not able to express themselves. [8,9] Dominance describes a scenario in which one group commands, controls, or prevails over others. [10] This study acknowledges that power involves the ownership and control of both tangible and intangible resources determining strategies of engagement within the healthcare teams. [5] The misunderstanding and conflicts that result from failure to appreciate roles and role boundaries, as well as the lack of a consultative approach in decision-making, are symptomatic of a power imbalance, which has a negative effect on patterns of collaboration. [6]

Healthcare leaders need to adopt approaches that ensure the balance of power in healthcare teams in order to achieve effective delivery of service. The balance of power among healthcare team members ensures good communication, shared responsibility, collaboration, and good coordination, all factors of good teamwork. [5,8] The healthcare leaders are responsible for shaping the organizational and working culture that informs how different individuals relate to each. [11] As posited by the transaction cost analysis theory, it is important for healthcare leaders to promote good relationship within healthcare teams by addressing resource concentration and control and by creating a culture that promotes shared decision-making and collaboration. [12] To this end, various researchers have examined the effective approaches that need to be adopted by the management to ensure balance of power. This research study analyzed data from relevant existing studies with the aim of developing a conclusive and in-depth understanding of the strategies that managers can use to address power dynamics in healthcare teams.

3ʳᵈ paragraph: Specific aspects especially in the last

Figure 7. The broad to specific approach in piecing together the information

Developing a Critical Analysis

The ability to critically assess the obtained information is based on the ability to recognize, analyze, and evaluate the reasoning and forms of argumentation in the articles. According to Klein (1996), critical analysis of the obtained literature is "giving reasons for one's beliefs and actions . . . recognizing reasons and conclusions, recognizing unstated assumptions, drawing conclusions, appraising evidence, and evaluating statements, judging whether conclusions are warranted" (p. 2). For one to carry out a critical analysis of the obtained information adequately, one needs to synthesize the work and succinctly pass judgment on the relative merits of the assessed research (Randolph, 2009). One should also identify limitations within the research and identify the possibility of taking the research further. The critical analysis of the assessed research exposes existing gaps, which is the main goal of the literature review.

Documenting the Different Steps of the Literature Review

For some research studies, such as the systematic review and meta-analysis, it is important to provide a detailed account of how the literature review was carried out. One of the tools that can be used to document the literature review process is the PRISMA (Preferred Reporting Items for Systematic Reviews and Meta-Analyses) chart (Appendix II). The PRISMA chart identifies all the records identified from the database search and those identified from other sources. The chart also describes the selection of the retrieved records by indicating the number of records that were eliminated at each stage of selection, along with the reasons for their elimination. Finally, the chart provides the total number of studies that were fully reviewed.

Checklist for the Assessment of an Effective Literature Review

Table 12 provides a checklist for evaluating the literature review.

Table 12

Checklist for Evaluating the Literature Review

Item	Description
Introduction	Check if the area of interest, the purpose of the study and review, and methods used in retrieval of article are highlighted.
Organization	Check if there is proper use of headings.
	Check if there is a logical flow of ideas and good transition between sections.
	Check if there are proper citations.
Description of the used articles	Check if there is a storyline that documents what was done, by whom, where and what was obtained, and the relevance to the study area.
Critical analysis	Check if each study is analyzed and critiqued.
	Check if there is analysis and critiquing across studies.
	Check if there is an identification of differences in argument and areas of convergence and gaps in knowledge
Conclusion	Check if there is a summary.
	Check if the summary links to the research methods.

CHAPTER 6: GUIDELINES FOR DEVELOPING AN EFFECTIVE RESEARCH DESIGN

The research design provides the blueprint for conducting research. Research designs are plans and procedures for research that span the decisions from broad assumptions to detailed methods of data collection and analysis (Creswell & Creswell, 2017). The selection of a research design is also based on the nature of the research problem or issue being addressed, the researchers' personal experiences, and the audience for the study. The research design is determined by the researcher's traditions and beliefs regarding the procedures of inquiry and the specific methods of data collection, analysis, and interpretation (Cone & Foster, 1993; Creswell & Creswell, 2017).

The choice and the nature of the research design that researchers adopt determine the quality of the findings in terms of validity, reliability, and generalizability. An appropriate methodology also provides the information needed by another competent scientist to repeat the work and helps in establishing the credibility of the obtained results (Baron, 2008). Without the use of an appropriate resign design, researchers may face problems in adequately answering the research question and in achieving smooth sailing in terms of conducting the various research operations (Cone & Foster, 1993; Kennedy-Clark, 2013). This chapter, therefore, seeks to describe the various aspects of the research design to provide guidelines that can be used in designing an appropriate research design that aligns with the research question. The aspects of the research methods that are discussed in this section include the following:

- Organization of the methods sections
- The language used in describing the methods
- Selection of the appropriate research design
- Addressing the challenges in data collection
- Addressing the challenges in the selection of a data analysis approach
- The influence of your personal experiences in the selection of research approach
- Assessment of whether the methodology is replicable, repeatable and robust

Organizing the Methods Section

To facilitate ease of assessment of the credibility of the presented findings based on the described methodology, researchers need to ensure that they use identical subheadings in the methods and the findings sections (Creswell & Creswell, 2017). Another strategy that can enhance the readers' easy following of the discussed methods is the use of introductory phrases or sentences in the methods section that relate to the aims.

The Language Used in Describing the Methods

Passive and Active Voice

The methodology should be written in the passive voice or active tense (Katz, 2009). The use of the passive tense emphasizes the action and removes emphasis from the doer of the action. The use of passive tense ensures that the action is more important than the doer. However, because some research requires the reader to be able to easily identify the doer of the action, the researcher should avoid passive voice and instead use active tense. The active tense recognizes the doer and action. For example, "The researcher invited the participants using posters" is written in the active tense. It should, however, be noted that active voice sounds repetitive, which has resulted in the choice being avoided by most researchers (Katz, 2009). The use of passive voice allows the researchers to incorporate old information into the methodology, which helps in enhancing the flow (Creswell & Creswell, 2017).

There are, however, problems that students need to look out for when using passive tense in the methodology. The major challenges that can render the methodology difficult to follow when written in passive tense are described below.

Very long subjects and a short passive verb right at the end. This is an example of a confusing use of passive tense: "Two RCT studies and four intervention studies collected from Google Scholar, as well one RCT article and three systematic review articles, retrieved from Pubmed, were used." This challenge can be addressed by placing both the subject and the verb in the first part of the sentence and the list of items at the end of the sentence: "Ten articles were used: Two RCT studies and four intervention studies collected from Google Scholar and one RCT article and three systematic review articles retrieved from Pubmed."

Repetition. The sentences should be abbreviated to avoid repetition.

Selection of the Appropriate Research Design

In this book, the research design will be discussed by categorizing them into quantitative and qualitative options. However, this does not mean that the author champions for separatist thinking in the selection of the research design (Kennedy-Clark, 2013). The author advocates for triangulation across the different levels of the study as a means of ensuring completeness of data and capturing as much information as possible about a particular phenomenon. Therefore, by highlighting qualitative and quantitative options, the author intends present the available options and describe how each can be used to ensure a wholesome approach to research.

The students should answer five main questions when choosing the appropriate research design:

I.   What kind of data will I gather?

II. How will I gather the data?

III. From whom will I gather the data?

IV. How will I analyze the data?

V.   How will I present data?

Upon examining the research question, the student may note that the question requires (a) a representative sample of many examples or (b) the variables to be examined in a controlled environment, which is typical of quantitative strategies. Some of the quantitative methodologies that can be employed include surveys, experimental designs, or intervention approaches (Kennedy-Clark, 2013). Alternatively, the student may note that the question requires a few examples that are studied in great depth, which is typical of qualitative strategies. Some of the qualitative methodologies that can be adopted are case studies and ethnography. Table 13 provides the answers to the above questions with a focus on quantitative and qualitative research approaches.

Table 13

Choosing the Appropriate Research Design

Question	Quantitative Research	Qualitative Research
What kind of data will you gather?	Scores, frequencies, rankings	Stories, perceptions, descriptions, narratives
How you will gather the data?	Test, questionnaire, observation schedule	Participant observations, open-ended interviews, document analysis
From whom you will gather the data?	Representative sample: random or stratified samples	Theoretical cases, purposive samples
How you will analyze the data?	Mean, mode, frequency, distribution, inferential statistics	Constant comparative analysis, grounded theory, discourse analysis
How you will present data?	Graphs, tables, diagrams	Participant quotations, observer field notes, concept maps

Challenges to Expect When Using a Qualitative Design

Here, the highlighted challenges are mainly those that are likely to be faced by the researchers who are exploring sensitive topics. The assessment of such challenges is meant to prepare the researchers to address such challenges. One of the challenges that the researchers can face is becoming *desensitized*. Listening to difficult stories from others can sometimes result in researchers not getting affected by them anymore (Dickson-Swift, James, Kippen, & Liamputtong, 2007). The lack of sensitivity to otherwise sensitive events can result in the researcher being viewed as alien, which has far-reaching effects on social relations. Researchers should be aware of the possibility of viewing extraordinary cases/events (e.g., such as stories of rape and other abuses) to be bizarrely ordinary. Desensitization can have the negative effect of estranging the researchers from their feelings (Dickson-Swift et al., 2007).

Another concern that qualitative researchers should be aware of is the *possibility of developing attachments*. Those researching sensitive topics have the risk of developing an emotional attachment to the participants, which can result in them thinking about them long after the completion of the research. Such thoughts can negatively affect the researchers in various ways, especially if they are not prepared to deal with such events.

Additionally, qualitative researchers are sometimes faced with the *feeling of vulnerability*, especially when the researcher is tasked with collecting data from people's homes. It is important to note that qualitative research can sometimes make you feel that you are learning things about yourself, which increases the feeling of vulnerability. Listening to the suffering of others sometimes exposes the researchers to disturbing thoughts about their mortality and vulnerability.

Researchers should also be aware that qualitative research could expose them to *feelings of guilt*. Qualitative researchers should be aware of the possibility of feeling guilty about the effects of the research on the participants. It should be noted that some of the sensitive information the respondents share can result in them recalling and reliving the events, which can have devastating emotional effects on the respondents. When researchers experience the participants' breakdowns during the interviews, they are sometimes made to think that they are using the participants as the means to achieve their ends. Researchers can also feel guilty about viewing the horrific stories shared by the participants as "good stuff" that will help them answer their research questions. A related challenge that qualitative researchers should be aware of is *exhaustion*. Collecting sensitive data through interviews can be emotionally and/or physically exhausting.

Finally, listening to difficult stories can sometimes leave researchers with a *feeling of responsibility*. For example, when interviewing rape victims who are vulnerable and cannot defend themselves, the stories can weigh heavily on the conscience of the researchers, and they can feel the need to act to protect the respondents.

How to address the challenges in qualitative research. It is important for researchers who choose qualitative designs to prepare adequately. They need to identify the approaches they can use to address the possible challenges that can be faced when collecting sensitive data using qualitative research. To address concerns about the challenges faced by the participants, researchers should be equipped with appropriate contact details of possible sources of *professional advice and support for those participants* (Dickson-Swift et al., 2007). It is also advisable for researchers to take a *risk assessment* for themselves and the research participants. The researchers also need to establish a support system that will help in the *debriefing* process. This support system can be made up of networks of colleagues, trusted friends, and family members who will counsel the researchers and help them cope with the challenges faced. The researchers should also consider building a *peer support program* that brings together a range of researchers (Dickson-Swift et al., 2007). The peer support program provides a forum for the researchers to share their experiences and develop a network of professional confidante. In particular, students need to take full advantage of professional supervision as a means of getting debriefing, mentoring, and skill development services. Researchers should also be advised to adopt *self-care strategies* as a means of protecting themselves against the physical and emotional harms. Some of the self-care strategies that can be adopted by researchers include debriefing, counseling, and scheduling rest breaks throughout the project. The researchers should leave enough space between interviews to help them process the stories they get from the data collection that might pose harm to their emotional well-being. Researchers also need to develop strategies to deal with emotions and emotional attachment and how to end the research relationship (Dickson-Swift et al., 2007).

Addressing the Challenges in Sample Selection

What Kind of Data Do I Need?

The answer to this question lies with the adopted research tradition. If you embrace objectivity in your research, as is the case with the positivist tradition, which is common in quantitative research, you need to have a *representative sample*. Otherwise, a *non-probability sample* is adequate for those who embrace subjectivity, as is the case with the interpretivist tradition, which is common in qualitative research.

How Do I Obtain a Representative Sample?

Researchers can obtain representative samples through probability sampling techniques, which include random, systematic, and stratified sampling. Random samples can be obtained through the use of a table of random numbers or a computer-generated random sample. A systematic random sample can be obtained by choosing the nth item from a listed set of items. Categorizing subjects and randomly selecting from the categories can also result in a stratified random sample.

How Do I Obtain a Non-Probability Sample?

Sampling can be carried out using the non-probability approach such as purposive, theoretical, convenient, snowball, and quota sampling. Purposive samples are selected based on the researcher's judgment and the objective of the study. Theoretical samples are selected based on the study's theoretical framework. A convenient sample is one that is easier to access and provides useful information. To obtain a snowball sample, the researcher asks the first subject to recommend another subject, who then recommends the next, and so on (Creswell & Creswell, 2017). Finally, a quota sample is made up of quotas for each of the categories the researcher wishes to represent.

Addressing the Challenges in Data Collection

Before suggesting the ways to address the challenges faced during data collection, it is important to first highlight the major challenges. The challenges presented in this book (and summarized in Table 14) are based on my experiences and the knowledge amassed from reading various articles and books.

Table 14

Summary of Challenges Faced in the Collection of Data

Nature of Challenges	List of Challenges
Researcher-related challenges	Uncooperative respondents
	Lack of experience, such as in carrying interviews
	Isolation from peers and other researchers
	Researcher fatigue
Participant-related challenges	Concerns over confidentiality
	Anxiety
	Handling distressed participants
	Literacy level of the participants
Challenges associated with data collection venue	Potential for disturbance
	The nearness of family members or significant others
Challenges associated with the adopted research design	Process of designing an interview guide
	Length of time need to observe the phenomenon of interest

Researcher-Related Challenges

The challenge associated with uncooperative respondents can be addressed by ensuring that the informed consent is used during the recruitment process to select participants who fully understand the study and their role in it. The use of informed consent also ensures that only those participants who are willing to take part in the study are selected. During the data collection process, the researcher can solve the issue of uncooperative respondents by allowing and encouraging the respondents to voice their concerns and to skip the questions they do not feel comfortable answering. The respondents should also be reminded of their freedom to quit the study at any time. The challenge associated with the lack of experience, such as that needed to effectively carry out interviews, can be addressed by ensuring that researchers carry out an extensive literature review on the topic to understand what other researchers have done. Depending on the chosen research design, the researcher can benefit from the knowledge of the respondents regarding the topic of interest. The researcher should allow the respondents to express their knowledge and understanding of the research phenomenon and lead the process of knowledge development. The challenge associated with isolation from peers and other researchers is a common problem that can be addressed through proper time management. The researcher needs to plan his/her time to ensure that there is time for private and social activities, which helps the researcher break from the research work and reconnect with friends and family. The challenge of researcher fatigue is also associated with the failure to adequately plan time or poor framing of the research question, which can lead to the need for extensive research within a limited period and with limited resources. In qualitative research, research fatigue can be limited by reducing the number of interviews conducted in a day. It is also advisable to take 30–60-minute breaks between interviews. Debriefing with a colleague or advisor after doing a set of interviews also helps address fatigue among researchers.

Participant-Related Challenges

The researcher should develop the questions based on the literacy level of the participants. There is also the need to pretest the data collection instrument among the nontarget population to identify the questions that the respondents may be uncomfortable with and restructure or delete the questions accordingly. The challenge associated with the concerns over confidentiality can be addressed during the recruitment phase; the researcher needs to disclose to participants the methods that will be used in securing their confidential information. The researcher needs to ensure that the research participants read and understand the content of the informed consent on data protection, privacy, and confidentiality. To ensure that the study adheres to ethical guidelines and to avoid concerns about confidentiality, the researcher should only recruit participants who express satisfaction with measures taken in the study to protect their privacy and confidentiality. The researcher should also allow participants who change their mind regarding their satisfaction with privacy and confidentiality measures to withdraw from the study. Concerns over privacy and confidentiality can also be addressed by allowing the participants to complete the data collection using alias names or by allowing the participants to use close cross-street addresses to their home instead of their exact addresses (Rimando et al., 2015). Ensuring that they understand their role in the study, how the information they provide will be protected and used, and their privacy and freedom to withdraw from the study without facing any consequences can address anxiety among the participants. It is also important to listen to the concerns of the participants and provide breaks from data collection for the participants to compose themselves and only continue with the data collection after determining the participants are ready and comfortable. Other techniques that can be used to manage anxiety among participants during data collection include incorporation of icebreakers before the interview, which helps make the participants at ease with the interviewer.

Challenges Associated with Data Collection Venue

Conducting the data collection in a neutral location helps address the challenges associated with the data collection venue. The chosen venue should be convenient and safe for both the participant and the researcher. Further, the location should allow participants to freely express themselves and the researcher to collect quality data.

Challenges Associated with the Adopted Research Design

Beginning with the framing of the research question, the researcher should ensure that the research design that will be adopted will not demand the use of data collection tools that are hard to develop. Whenever possible, the research design that is adopted should allow the use of existing tools whose reliability and validity have been established (Creswell & Creswell, 2017). If this is not possible, the researcher should use triangulation to help address the possible challenges that can be faced when developing a data collection tool from scratch. Triangulation calls for the researchers to immerse themselves in the existing relevant literature to identify ways to help direct the development of data collection tools. It is best practice for the researcher to test the data collection tools to ensure their fit and reliability for the study.

Other Challenges
What If I Am Dealing with Hard-to-Reach Data Sources?

Students sometimes choose a research question that requires them to sample and collect data from hard-to-reach participants, such as the houseless people; the lesbian, gay, bisexual, and transgender communities; individuals with rare medical conditions; people who use illegal substances; and the low prevalent group in a given population (e.g., Aboriginal people). The challenge that such researchers face as a result is the difficulty in accumulating large enough samples using random population samples (Bonevski et al., 2014). Attempts to use probability sampling on such hard-to-reach populations tend to be a time- and cost-inefficient strategy. To address this challenge, researchers are advised to adopt alternative sampling approaches, such as the non- probability options, which include snowballing, social networking or respondent-driven recruitment, venue-based time-location sampling, targeted sampling, capture-recapture, adaptive sampling, and oversampling of low prevalence population subgroups (Bonevski et al., 2014). However, the challenge with the use of these suggested sampling approaches is selection bias and gatekeeper bias, which can limit validity, especially in quantitative research. Researchers can use these approaches, however, because they are less concerned with representativeness and generalizability (Bonevski et al., 2014).

Another option is to involve community organizations to help access the specific socially disadvantaged groups. The researcher then uses a convenience sampling approach to select the accessed participants (Hoppitt et al., 2012). To reduce the cost associated with recruiting members of the hard-to-reach population, researchers are advised to collaborate with community organizations and religious groups. Other available options that can be adopted by the researcher include direct mail, community outreach, and recruitment through a health education council (Keyzer et al., 2005).

What If the Participants Have Low Literacy Levels and Language Use?

The collection of data can also be affected by the inability of the respondents to understand the language that has been used in a data collection tool such as a questionnaire. Researchers can address this problem by simplifying the readability of the study materials by using simpler language (Bonevski et al., 2014). Alternatively, researchers are encouraged to translate materials into other, more common languages (Bonevski et al., 2014; McMillan et al., 2009). If the problem persists, researchers are encouraged to use bilingual research assistants (Anderson et al., 2009; Eakin et al., 2006). Other approaches that can be used to address the inability of the respondents to understand the language used are to involve culturally trained and skilled field workers (Flory & Emanuel, 2004). Researchers can also opt to use locals or peers to conduct fieldwork, which can also help to address mistrust (Hing, Breen, & Gordon, 2010; Ryan, Kofman, & Aaron, 2011). Sometimes, the use of third parties, such as the hiring of locals or the use of bilingual research assistants, can introduce other problems, such as confidentiality concerns and cost-effectiveness of the research. To address such challenges, the researcher should change the approach used in asking a question by adopting approaches such as the use of photo voice, which allows the researcher to use pictures and photos to tell the story (Hergenrather, Rhodes, Cowan, Bardhoshi, & Pula, 2009).

What If the Respondents Cannot Access the Data Collection Tool?

Sometimes the research question requires the researcher to collect data from a hard-to-reach population that may not be able to access the data collection tool (e.g., inaccessibility to landline or mobile phone for telephone interviews). In such a scenario, the researchers can be hard-pressed to find an alternative because they do not want to lose the hard-to-find respondents. The researcher can solve such problems by incorporating other forms of data collection, such as face-to-face door interviews or online surveys (Bonevski et al., 2014; Shebl et al., 2009). However, researchers should be cautious when supplementing the existing data collection with another form of data collection (e.g., supplementing online questionnaires with face-to-face interviews) because there is a high risk of introducing very low kappa agreement scores due to the lack of equivalence in the responses obtained (Bonevski et al., 2014).

Addressing the Challenges in the Selection of a Data Analysis Approach

The answer to which data analysis approach to use depends on the research question and the chosen research design (see the Chapter 3 and the beginning of this chapter for further information on the association between the research question and research design).

Analysis of Quantitative Data

The data analysis approaches that can be adopted by quantitative researchers involve the conversion of data to numeric forms followed by statistical analysis. First, the data needs to be prepared by editing, identifying missing data, coding and data entry, and data transformation. Data editing involves the inspection of the data for completeness and consistency. The data can then be inspected for missing data, using approaches such as simple descriptive statistics. Standard practice is that questionnaires that are missing more than 10% of the total responses should be eliminated. The coding of data involves the assigning of a numeric value (e.g., male = 1, female = 2) to the data to facilitate the data analysis using data analysis software such as SPSS. Data transformation involves the changing of the data into a new format, such as the changing of a 10-point Likert scale to a 5-point scale.

Data Analysis Options for Quantitative Data

The number of variables determines the quantitative data analysis approach. For a single variable, univariate statistical analysis can be adopted, the bivariate analysis is adopted for two variables, and the multivariate analysis is adopted for the research question with several variables. The univariate statistics are focused on describing the variable by explaining the distribution (frequency distribution), central tendency (mean, mode, and median), and dispersion (range, variance, and standard deviation). The bivariate and multivariate focus on explanation. Examples of bivariate analysis include linear regression analysis, correlation (relationship), distribution, t-test, a one-way Analysis of variance (ANOVA), and scatter plot. (The selection of the appropriate bivariate analysis is outside the scope of this book) Examples of multivariate analysis include the MANOVA (multiple analysis of variance), Analysis of covariance (ANCOVA), cluster analysis, hierarchical linear modeling, logistic regression, and logistic analysis.

Common Analytical Software Used in the Analysis of Quantitative Data

Microsoft Excel. The benefits of Excel are that it is free of charge, includes everything in one program, and can be password secured. However, the software is limited by slow speeds when analyzing large files, has a limited number of rows and columns, and is vulnerable to viruses.

Microsoft Access. Also free and easy to access and use, Access is limited by a low level of interactivity and difficulties in dealing with large databases.

SPSS. The use of SPSS is common due to the advantages associated with the software, such as its broad coverage of formulas and statistical routines; the fact that it allows importing data files from other programs; and the fact that it is annually updated to increase sophistication. Its use, however, is limited by its high cost, limited license duration, and confusion among the different versions due to regular updates.

Data Analysis Options for Qualitative Data

Qualitative data analysis is based on interpretative philosophy. The deductive and the inductive approaches are the two approaches in qualitative data analysis. The deductive approach is based on the use of the research questions to group the data, which is then followed by the location of the similarities and differences. The deductive approach is commonly used when the time and resources are limited or when qualitative research is a smaller component of a larger quantitative study. The inductive approach involves the use of the emergent framework to group the data and then look for relationships. The inductive approach is used when qualitative research is a major design of the inquiry. The analysis of the qualitative data occurs in five major steps. The first is the *organization of data* through transcription, translation, cleaning, and labeling of data. The second step is the *identification of a framework*, which means the identification of the coding plan. The framework is important in structuring, labeling, and defining data. The third step is *sorting of the data into the framework*, which involves the coding of data, modification of the framework, and the accurate and appropriate entry of the data. The fourth step is the *use of the framework in descriptive analysis*, which involves the arrangement of the responses in categories and the identification of the recurrent themes. The final step is the *second-order analysis*, in which the researcher identifies patterns in the data and the respondent clusters and develops the sequence of events. The data are then searched to answer the research questions and, finally, the hypothesis is developed and tested. The final step only applies to explanatory qualitative analysis, which is guided by the research question. With the exploratory qualitative analysis, this is guided by the data, the data analysis stops at step 4.

Examples of commonly used software analytical software in the analysis of qualitative data are Atlasti6.0 , HyperRESEARCH2, MaxQDA, TheEthnography5.08, QSRN6, QSRNvivo, WeftQDA, and Open code 3.4.

The Influence of Your Personal Experiences in the Selection of the Research Approach

Consider your training and experiences in selecting the appropriate design. Someone with experience in technical, scientific writing, and statistics is likely to be comfortable choosing a quantitative design. Researchers who are uncomfortable with challenging accepted approaches among some faculty through the use of qualitative and advocacy/participatory approaches also gravitate toward quantitative designs, which are the traditional mode of research due to their carefully worked out procedures and rules. However, researchers who engage in personal interviews and enjoy writing in a literary way are likely not to be comfortable with the qualitative design. Researchers, who like being innovative and work more within researcher-designed frameworks, tend to gravitate toward a qualitative design. However, researchers who prefer the flexibility of qualitative inquiry and structure of quantitative research tend to use mixed methods.

Assessment of Whether the Methodology is Replicable, Repeatable, and Robust

Replicable

Quantitative researchers mainly need replicable research. The indicators of replicable research include the inclusion of control experiments, repeated analyses, and repeated experiments. Sampling also enhances the replicability of a given research.

Repeatable

A repeatable methodology gives enough detail so other researchers can carry out the same research. Researchers are therefore advised to provide sufficient details about the instrument used, study participants and how they were recruited, the procedure used in the collection of data, and how the data were manipulated and analyzed.

Robust

Robust research is one that has sufficient data points that facilitate the determination of data reliability. Researchers, therefore, need to ensure that the findings of the manuscript that is submitted for publishing are based on sufficient data. Researchers should also examine the presence of bias, especially bias that might have been nullified by the control experiments.

Checklist for the Assessment of an Effective Research Design

There are sets of best practices that a researcher needs to demonstrate adherence to for a manuscript to be accepted and published. Some of the best practice guidelines are related to ethical standards, the health and safety of all participants, and standard guideline that governs different types of research, such as Consolidated Standards Of Reporting Trials (CONSORT) statement for reporting randomized trials. The researcher needs to determine the best practices that are related to the adopted research design and the field of interest. Table 15 provides a summary of the key guidelines that guide the development of the research design.

Table 15

Checklist for the Evaluation of the Research Design

Item	Description
Is the problem statement provided?	Check if the problem statement is stated along with the background statistics.
Is the literature review provided?	Check if the research design is grounded within the existing literature.
	Check if the definition of terms, variables, data collection tools, and sampling approaches is evidence-based.
Is the hypothesis stated?	Check if the relationship between the variables is hypothesized.
Are the variables described?	Check if the DV and IV and the intervening variables (if any) are provided.
	Check if the variable is measurable.
	Check if the unit of analysis is provided.
Are the indicators provided?	Check if the indicators (objective, event-based, subjective, or proxy) are described.
Are the levels of measurement provided?	Check if the scale is described as being nominal, ordinal, or interval.
Is the sampling approached described?	Check if the type of sampling is identified.
	Check if the sampling approach is supported by literature.
	Check if the approach used to determine the sample size is described and supported by the existing literature.

	Check if the approach used in the recruitment of the respondents is identified and fully described.
Are the methods well described?	Check if the methods are identified and the rationale for the choice is provided.
	Check if the approach used in disqualifying other candidate methods is provided.
Is the data collection approach well described?	Check if the data collection method is identified and justified.
	Check if the data collection tool (s) is identified and that rationale is provided, along with the validity and reliability.
Is the data analysis described?	Check if the approach used in the presentation of findings is provided.
	Check if the DV and IV and the approaches used to analyze data relating to each research question are identified.
	Check if the test for the reliability and the validity of the developed data collection tool is provided.

CHAPTER 7: EFFECTIVE PRESENTATION OF

THE FINDINGS

The analysis of the obtained data can yield several findings. Researchers should be able to sift through the numerous results and identify the results that answer the research questions. The presentation of findings in dissertations and theses vary slightly from the approach used in the presentation of findings in a manuscript. Normally, the length of an article is restricted, which means the number of findings that are generated from a typical research project cannot be accommodated in a single article (Fah and Aziz, 2006). Researchers need to be concise but still be able to articulate clearly the results in a manner that can be understood by the target audience. The researchers should have the ability to select the findings that are worth presenting, and they should be able to package the information effectively. This chapter provides guidelines on how to present the findings in the manuscript to enhance the possibility of positive publication outcome. The aspects of the presentation of the findings that are addressed in this chapter include the following:

- General considerations for organizing the findings
- Use of text in the presentation of the findings

- Use of tables

- Use of graphs

- Presentation of statistics

- Checklist for the evaluation of presentation of the findings

General Considerations for Organizing the Findings

The presentation of the findings should be simple, should proceed from general to specific findings, should be geared toward answering the research questions, and should be described using the past tense.

Use of Text in the Presentation of the Findings

The text is used to describe the findings that are presented in the tables and figures. The text should be able to highlight the data and provide the interpretation, which makes reading the findings less difficult. However, researchers should avoid the repetition of the information contained in the tables and figures in the written text (Fah & Aziz, 2006). Instead, they should only highlight the most important results in the text. Researchers should avoid using colorful words when describing the results but instead use the data to convey the information. Words such as remarkably, clearly evident, extremely, and obviously need to be avoided (Fah & Aziz, 2006). The examples below show how text should and should not be used in describing the findings.

The Text Used for Interpretation

This example lacks the interpretation of findings: "The average BMI of 20 teens before the intervention was 28.1 kg/m2 and was 23.1 kg/m2 after the intervention." However, this example shows how to interpret the findings: "The average BMI of 20 teens decreased from 28.1 kg/m2 to 23.1 kg/m2 after the intervention."

Use of Unnecessary Words

This example contains the unnecessary words: "It is clearly evident that the average BMI of 20 teens reduced from 28.1 kg/m2 to 23.1 kg/m2 after the intervention." The preferred way to report the findings is this: "The average BMI of 20 teens decreased from 28.1 kg/m2 to 23.1 kg/m2 after the intervention."

Use of Tables

Researchers should use tables to present the numerical values that answer the research question. The use of tables allows the researcher to summarize large sets of data. The data presented in the tables can also be easily compared. Features of well-prepared tables include the title, columns, rows, and footnotes. The title should be brief and specific; it needs to provide a summary of the variables in the columns and rows (Grange, 1998). Similar data should be presented in the columns (Fah & Aziz, 2006). The footnotes should be used to enhance the clarity of the information presented in the table. The footnotes are usually listed at the bottom of the tables and can be identified using the abbreviations such as *, †, ‡, §, ‖, ¶, **, ††, or #. The abbreviations used should be standard throughout the section.

To enhance the clarity of the information presented in the body of the tables, the researcher needs to ensure that standardized units and number of decimals are used. The researcher should also adopt a systematic approach for the presentation of dates and timing. Further, the fewest number of zeros possible should be used. For example, instead of having lines that delineate every cell, three lines can be used: Two at the top to show the column heading and one to demarcate table end. A symbol such as an asterisk (*) can be used to enhance the neatness of the presentation when highlighting the significant values (Fah & Aziz, 2006).

Use of Graphs

Graphs are best suited to show trends in the presented data. They are also used to avoid a lengthy description of the findings in the text by providing visual emphasis. They should incorporate a title, figure legend, and footnotes. The features of the figures have the same characteristics as those of the tables (Fah & Aziz, 2006). Categorical data can be presented using bar charts, but 3-D charts and graphs should be avoided because they make the reading of the values in the Y-axis cumbersome. The presentation of the values that change over time is best done using the line graphs. Researchers should, however, practice caution when using graphs because there is a likelihood of losing the precision of the values that exist in the tables (Grange, 1998). Researchers need to focus on what they intend to communicate: if the intention is to show trends, graphs should be used; otherwise, the communication of precise values should be done using tables.

Presentation of Statistics

Most of the manuscripts that fail to be accepted by the journals fail because of errors in the presentation of the statistics. Researchers need to ensure the reported statistics are not only comprehensible by the average reader but also sufficiently rigorous to withstand the critique of experts (Fah & Aziz, 2006; Ransohoff & Lang, 1997). To facilitate proper reporting of statistics, researchers need to have a good understanding of the meaning of the statistics. Researchers with a poor understanding of statistics are encouraged to seek help from statisticians.

Some statistics are best presented in the text, such as the mean and standard deviation, median, and normality testing (Ransohoff & Lang, 1997). However, more complicated statistical tests that involve the assessment of several variables are best displayed in tables, followed with brief prose. Researchers need to ensure that the p-values are quoted and correctly interpreted. For values with insignificant statistical values, the researcher should avoid indicating $p > 0.05$ but instead specify the exact p-values. Where possible, the researcher should present the 5% confidence intervals (95% CI) along with the p-values (Fah & Aziz, 2006).

Components of the Discussion of the Results

The discussion should be provided as a stand-alone chapter after the results chapter. The components of the discussion chapter are these:

Restatement of the purpose of the research. The discussion should start with the restatement of what is being researched.

Consolidation of the findings and linking with previous research. The next step is to summarize methods, findings, and claims with references to the relevant existing literature.

Recommendations. The discussion should highlight how the obtained findings link with the wider world and future research. The researcher should identify the areas that need further research.

Implications. The implications refer to how the findings relate to the wider world. The findings can be discussed based on how it influences the practice (practice implications) or it influences future research (research implication).

Concluding restatement. The concluding statements should be made up of reiteration of the overall findings and claims.

Checklist for the Evaluation of the Presentation of the Findings

Table 16 describes the checklist that should be considered when developing the presentation of the findings section.

Table 16

Checklist for the Evaluation of the Findings Section

Item	Description
Do the findings address the research question?	Check if the various aspects of the research questions are adequately addressed.
Is the section well organized?	Check if the broader findings are presented first, followed by the specific findings.
	Check if the headings of the results align with the objectives/research questions and the methods.
Is the text well used?	Check if the text is used to interpret the findings.
	Check if there is any use of unnecessary words.
Are the tables well presented?	Check if the data in the table columns refer to similar variables.
	Check if the required number of lines are used.
	Check if the title, footnote columns, and the rows are well labeled.
Are the figures well presented?	Check if the data are presented using the appropriate figures.
	Check if the title and footnotes are well labeled.
Are the statistics well presented?	Check if the p-values are correctly reported.
	Check if the p-values are correctly interpreted.
	Check if the statistics are comprehensible to the average reader.
	Check if the statistics are correct.

CHAPTER 8: FORMULATION OF AN EFFECTIVE ABSTRACT

Abstracts provide the summary of the article; they are usually the second most important part after the title that the reader assesses to determine the suitability of the article to their research interests. Thus, formulation of a good abstract is an important undertaking for every researcher. This chapter provides guidelines for novice researchers and students who have questions on how to write an abstract and what to include in it. The aspects of the abstract that are addressed in this chapter include the following:

I.   Definition of a good abstract

II. Importance of a good abstract

III. The Preferred structure of abstracts

IV. Summary of steps to take in writing an effective abstract

What Is a Good Abstract?

Knowing what a good abstract is important because it guides what needs to be included in the abstract. The following is a summary of a good/effective abstract;

- Made of a single or multiple standalone paragraphs

that are coherent and concise

- Provides an accurate, complete, and concise description of the different parts of the research paper (e.g., background/introduction, purpose of the study, methodology, result, discussion, and conclusion), usually in the order in which they appear in the paper

- Made of well-connected ideas

- Does not introduce any idea that is not covered in the paper

- The first sentence of the abstract should be compelling and engaging to the reader (Huston & Choi, 2017)

Why Is It Important to Have a Good Abstract?

Researchers need to take time to formulate an effective abstract for several reasons. First, most readers only read the abstract due to time constraints and base their judgment on whether it is worth spending time reading the entire manuscript. Second, for readers who do not have full access to the entire paper, the decision to purchase a paper is solely based on the abstract. Third, good abstracts enhance the visibility of the article.

What Is the Preferred Structure of Abstracts?

The answer to this question lies with the instructions provided by the selected journal. It is best practice to consult the journal before writing the abstract. Some journals provide a list of questions or headings for authors to respond to in writing their abstracts. For journals that do not provide explicit instruction on the structure of the abstract, the researcher should analyze articles that have been published in the journal to determine the generally accepted approach. Although abstracts are typically made up of 250 to 350 words, researchers should consult the selected journal's instructions and guidelines on the preferred number of words.

To develop writing competence, students should read various abstracts and analyze the structure and how the information is connected. The flow of the information in the abstract is based on how well the researcher understands the content of the research paper. Although an abstract requires the researcher to include the various sections of the paper, researchers should spend more time on unique contributions of the research and how the findings were obtained. The example below shows an abstract that was published in the *International Journal of*

Healthcare Management by the author of this book. The first sentence of the abstract provides background information. The second sentence provides the purpose of the study, and the third sentence provides a summary of the research approach. The fourth, fifth, and sixth sentences summarize the major findings of the article. Finally, the last sentence provides the overall conclusion of the study.

The US healthcare sector is among leading globally in the incorporation of advanced technologies in its operations. This study evaluated existing data to understand how technological advancement in the US healthcare sector has impacted the cost of healthcare services and patient satisfaction. The study was based on a quantitative analysis of 24 existing studies selected from various electronic databases. The results indicate a significant increase in the cost of healthcare service due to technology adoption and other factors. Increase in cost due to technology adoption is evident in the area of diagnosis (63%, $P = 0.002$) and patient monitoring (51%, $P = 0.021$). A significantly higher percentage was found, of patients that believe the adoption of advanced technologies leads to improved quality in diagnostic procedures (67%, P = 0.042), monitoring (79%, P = 0.004), and data keeping (85%, P = 0.032). Strategies need to be developed to manage costs associated with technological adoption while ensuring the delivery of quality services (Okpala, 2018).

Summary of Steps to Take in Writing an Effective Abstract

1. Do a thorough reading of the research paper to develop a summarized approach in your mind.

2. Based on the conceptualized summary, develop a rough abstract without looking back at your research paper. Ensure you have captured the different sections of the paper, but avoid copying and pasting key sentences from your article.

3. Revise the initial draft to address the limitation in the structure and flow, remove unnecessary information, add important details that had been left out, reduce wordiness, and correct grammatical mistakes and sentence structure.

4. Carefully proofread your final draft.

PART 2: BASIC GUIDELINES ON JOURNAL SELECTION: THE PACKAGING OF THE RESEARCH MATERIAL TO A MANUSCRIPT

CHAPTER 9: GUIDELINES ON JOURNAL SELECTION

The process of publishing completed research is systematic and involves the collaboration between the editor, reviewers, and the author. The demands across various journals vary. Some journals have stringent demands and rules and longer periods of article review, which can prolong the process of publishing the article. The researchers, therefore, need to identify the journal that fits their requirement and the available time. This chapter provides guidelines to students and novice researchers on how to go about publishing their research. The aspects of publishing addressed in this chapter include the following:

- What a researcher should do to successfully publish the manuscript
- Selection of the journal
- What to consider when selecting the journal

What a Researcher Should Do to Successfully Publish the

Manuscript

Novice researchers and students to optimize their publication outcomes can use various strategies. The strategies are listed below:

- Develop a critical and strong framework for manuscript writing by reviewing manuscripts for fellow researchers and journals.

- Carry out due diligence and understand the quality assurance criteria that referees and editors use to be able to plan the research well and produce quality writing.

- Select the journal earlier during the initial stages of research to package the paper to meet the journal's specifications and maximize the chances of acceptance.

- Pay keen attention to the referees' reports and address all the concerns raised by the editor and the referees. Demonstrate to the journal editor how you have improved the manuscript based on the journal referees' reports.

- Cultivate honesty, an eye for detail, and patience when writing the manuscript.

Selection of the Journal

As indicated, the ease of publishing and the time it takes to publish vary across different journals. It should also be noted that the size of the audience, professional prestige, and rewards vary across the different journals. It is therefore important for researchers to choose the journal that fits their requirements.

When Is the Appropriate Time to Choose the Journal?

At the beginning of the research is the best time to start identifying the appropriate journal for the research. Researchers should have identified the journal by the time of writing the introduction and discussion sections (Huston & Choi, 2017; Testa, 2009).

Should I Choose Only One Journal?

According to guidelines to publishing scientific research by Huston and Choi (2017), it is not advisable to select only one journal. Rather, Huston and Choi argue that one should select at least three and a maximum of five journals. The chosen journals should be ordered in terms of journal impact factor. As will be discussed later in this chapter, the selection of three to five journals is important in the event of rejection of the manuscript by the first journal selection.

What to Consider When Selecting the Journal
Time Taken to Publish

When selecting the appropriate journals for your manuscript, it is important to consider your preferred time of publication (i.e., how long you are willing to wait before the paper is published). The issue of time is particularly vital for researchers whose progress in their career or academic progress depends on the successful and timely publication of their manuscripts. However, it should be noted that the issue of time limitation when selecting a given journal can be addressed by planning, executing, and completing your research early enough to give sufficient time between publishing and your academic or career timelines (Guyatt & Haynes, 2006). Thus, researchers should identify the journal early enough and be familiar with its publishing demands to plan the research and prepare in advance (Huston & Choi, 2017).

Researchers need to check on the time taken by the journals to publish the received submission. The average time to publication can be obtained from the journal website.

Desired Professional Prestige

Another factor to consider is the desired professional prestige. Journals with high prestige are often strict and only allow the publication of the papers that have attained set standards. Researchers interested in such journals should ensure that their research approach, the topic they choose, presentation of the data, quality of writing, and discussion of the findings adhere to every set regulation (García et al., 2014).

Access to the Desired Audience

Another factor that is important to consider is the access to the desired audience (Huston & Choi, 2017). The journal you choose should allow access to your target audience. For example, if your target audience is upcoming researchers in developing countries, it makes more sense to publish the article in open access journals because most of the target audience may lack access to paid/subscription journals. If the target is a large section of the population distributed across different academic and geographical divides, the researcher should avoid journals with limited distribution. New journals are likely to have a limited audience.

Is it peer-reviewed?

Another factor that needs to be considered is whether the candidate journals have peer reviewers (García et al., 2014). The peer-review process is important for establishing the quality of your work and the development of your research profile. Thus, it is advisable for all researchers to consider publishing their work in peer-reviewed journals (Dougherty, Freda, Kearney, Baggs, & Broome, 2011).

The Scope and Aims of the Journal

Every journal publishes its aims and scope on its website, and the scope and aims of the journal influence the readership. It is important to check the described scope and aims to determine whether they are aligned with the aims of your study (Huston & Choi, 2017). The likelihood of your paper being accepted by the selected journal also depends on the articles that you have cited in the introduction and the discussion sections of your paper. Thus, researchers should read their introduction and discussion to develop a mind map of the frequently cited articles and related journals. Such information will aid in the selection of the journal that is likely to accept the work. However, as previously stated, the selection of the journal should occur before the writing of the introduction and the discussion (García et al., 2014). This is important because it will ensure that the articles used in completing the sections are from the preferred journal.

Journal Impact Factor

One of the factors that a researcher should consider when selecting a given journal is the quality of the journal and its contribution to the research in the discipline of interest (García et al., 2014). It should be noted that there is no easy way of determining the quality of a given journal and differentiating between different journals. One of the proposed approaches is to use the Journal Impact Factor, which is based on the number of times an article that is published in a journal of interest is cited within a given period (García et al., 2014). The Journal Impact Factor for a given year is described as the mean number of times articles published in the journal in the two previous years have been cited in that year. The impact factor, therefore, simply gives the average recent use of the articles in the journal. The other measure that researchers can use to judge the quality of the journal of interest is the Journal Immediacy Index, which describes how rapidly the average articles are used in the journal. The Journal Immediacy Index is obtained by dividing the total number of articles that are cited in a year by the total number of articles that are published in that journal in that year.

Free or Paid Journals

Some journals charge fees for publishing manuscripts. Thus, researchers need to be aware of the terms of publication to avoid unforeseen inconveniences. For journals that charge fees for publishing manuscripts, researchers need to establish the criteria used to determine the total cost of publishing and plan appropriately (Dougherty et al., 2011).

CHAPTER 10: PACKAGING OF A QUALITY

MANUSCRIPT

After the completion of the research and all the sections

of the paper (introduction, literature, methods, findings,

discussion, and conclusion) have been written, the researcher

should then repackage the information into a quality thesis based

on the journal requirements. For the case of students, this involves

the repackaging of the vast information contained in the thesis to

fit the requirements of the selected Journal. Important factors to

consider when developing the manuscript include clarity,

relevance, and avoidance of plagiarism. This chapter discusses

these features of quality manuscripts:

- Clarity of manuscripts

- Relevance of manuscripts

- Avoidance of plagiarism

- Assessing the quality of a manuscript

-

Clarity of Manuscripts

Novice researchers and students often fail to differentiate

between thesis and manuscript writing and thus end up lacking logical clarity. Manuscripts with a high level of clarity tend to have a higher chance of being published. This section provides a discussion of the strategies for achieving clarity in manuscripts.

Strategies for Achieving Clarity

Carefully plan every section of research. Researchers who intend to publish their findings need to have foresight from the early stages of research planning, execution, and writing (Young, 2002). Thus, researchers need to consider the various aspects of manuscript writing during the initial stages of study design. The creation and the use of program resources, survey instruments, or other written products need to consider the requirements that should be met for the paper to be published in the selected journal. This further demonstrates why it is important to select the journals during the early stages of project design. It is important to ensure that the materials that are used in research are easily understandable, grammatically and mechanically correct, and free from misspellings and inconsistencies.

Develop an outline and stick to it. The use of an outline helps a writer organize thoughts before writing. The outline also enhances clarity by breaking down the topic, which can help identify potential weaknesses in the argument. The outline helps the writer identify the supporting details that are required to make the discussion of the major aspects compelling and complete. The outline also ensures that researchers remain focused on the subject and avoid the back and forth in writing, which can be confusing to the readers.

Ensure coherence on both macro and micro levels. A coherent manuscript should flow like a story where the different parts contribute meaningfully to the whole. Researchers should therefore ensure that although the different sections convey unique information and are standalone, they should be interlinked by consistent concepts and thought processes. The different sections and subsections of the manuscript need to be identified using clear and appropriate headings and subheadings. It is also important to avoid redundancy in writing (Young, 2002); researchers should avoid reformulating the same points across the different sections of the manuscript.

To enhance coherence, the paragraphs should be kept as short as possible while ensuring that unnecessary breaking up of information is avoided. Repacking the content rather than breaking up the paragraphs can shorten long paragraphs. Each of the paragraphs should have a topic sentence that helps readers digest the dense and complicated content, while transitions link the subsequent paragraphs to the information within the paragraphs (Caelli, Ray, & Mill, 2003).

When numbering the sections and sub-sections within the manuscript, it is important to be consistent. Enhanced coherence can also be achieved through the use of a consistent language when referring to a specific item or phenomenon. Choose the definition to adopt a specific phenomenon, and stick to it. Caution should be exercised when using synonyms because there is a high risk of repetition (Caelli et al., 2003).

Coherence is also achieved through the adoption of parallel construction of the different sections, such as the headings and the paragraphs. Further, parallelism in grammar should be adopted through the development of the sentences with the same grammatical structure. The content also needs to be organized logically. The ordering of the items needs to adopt a logical order either through alphabetical or chronological ordering (Caelli et al., 2003).

Proofreading. Proofreading of the completed work is important in identifying and correcting grammatical and structural errors. The researcher should read the paper and correct mistakes.

Additionally, it is advisable to have a colleague read your manuscript, preferably a colleague who is not familiar with your research. Having a different person read your work helps identify areas that might confuse the readers. Your colleague will also help judge the quality of your work and suggest areas that need to be improved (Young, 2002).

Choice of Language

Language is a powerful tool for conveying information. Avoid offensive language and use accepted language when describing racial and ethnic identities of study participants. Do not use jargon and buzzwords. It is also best to avoid ambiguous or illogical comparisons (Messuri, 2015). To get a grasp of the preferred language, researchers should read journals and note the language used in the description of the research design, data analysis, and discussions.

Achieving Clarity through a Consistent Flow of Ideas

Consistency is one of the most important features of research writing and reporting. Students need to ensure consistency in the content, structure, and language used in their research and manuscript. Ensuring consistency in research writing avoids sidetracking into areas that are not aligned with the topic (Pierson, 2004). Students and novice researchers also need to embrace consistency as a timesaving technique. (More time-saving approaches will be discussed later in this book.) By adopting consistency in research, the researcher avoids problems such as collection of data that do not address the title and the study purpose and the back and forth in writing caused by the need to clarify inconsistencies (Pierson, 2004).

Building consistency between the problem statement, title, purpose, and research questions. The problem statement, title, purpose, and research questions form the first part of the manuscript that the readers encounter. Establishing consistency in the problem statement, title, purpose, and research questions makes the logical arrangement of the other sections of the manuscript attainable (Oliver, 2011). To achieve consistency in the problem statement, title, purpose, and research questions, researchers need to ensure they identify the concepts or constructs of interest. The identified concepts of interest, then, make the basis upon which the literature is used to develop the problem statement and purpose. The identification of the concepts, as indicated earlier in this book, is based on the developed research question. Although the title may be continuously updated throughout the writing process, it is important in the early stages of the research because it provides the keywords and relationships that guide the formulation of the problem, purpose, and research questions (Pierson, 2004). Therefore, one feature of a good title is its consistency with the other parts of the research. To ensure consistency between the title and the problem statement and the purpose of the research, there is a need to ensure the *why* and *what* aspects of the sections are fine-tuned. The *why* of the title provides the need and importance of the research. Thus, it is important to ensure that the title justifies the importance of the study. Providing a justification of the study in the title can ensure this and verify the problem statement and purpose of the research builds on that justification (Neale & West, 2015).

Relevance of the Manuscript

The relevance of the manuscript is a rarely discussed topics in the preparation of the manuscript, yet it is one of the most important considerations by the editor when deciding on whether the manuscript should be sent to the referees. It is the responsibility of the editor to ensure that the manuscripts that are accepted are relevant to the audience that the journal serves. It is also the responsibility of the researcher to ensure that he/she chooses a journal whose aims and scope agrees with the study objectives and the research questions (Ali, 2010). This section provides an in-depth description of manuscript relevance and what the researchers should focus on to ensure that the manuscript is relevant.

What Determines Relevance?

Understanding what determines the relevance of the manuscript is important in designing and the writing of the manuscript. In scientific research and journals, the mission of the journal, its scope, and the work of its readership determine the manuscript's relevance.

What Are the Conditions for Relevance?

The relevance of the content and the research question. The editor and the reviewers judge the relevance of the manuscript based on its propriety for the journal, which indicates the suitability of the manuscript to the readership's interest and the focus of the journal. The propriety of the manuscript for the journal is based on the determination of the extent to which the topic of the manuscript and its research questions overlap or touch the scope of the journal (Dougherty et al., 2011).

For example, say the editors ask, *Does the topic of the manuscript address some sections of interest to the journal focus?* Irrespective of the quality of writing and impact of the findings, the editors, with the help of the reviewers, can still reject the manuscript out of hand if its topic does not overlap with the focus of the journal. It is therefore important for researchers to thoroughly examine the foci of the journals of interest to determine whether they overlap with the aim of the study (Dougherty et al., 2011). The researchers should determine the importance of the manuscript to the journal through the judgment of the magnitude of the overlap that exists between the manuscript topic and focus of the journal.

The manuscripts that are regarded as being important (based on their propriety to the focus of the journal) are subjected to further scrutiny to determine their relevance within the journal's field of interest. The editors use various aspects of the manuscript topic and subject in judging its importance. One consideration is whether the manuscript addresses what is considered a serious problem. The manuscripts that focus on real problems that are within the journal's area of interest are considered to be relevant. Such manuscripts should be able to provide practical solutions to the identified problem (Ali, 2010). Apart from establishing the fact that the research problem is serious, the editors also assess whether the problem is common. The editors will consider manuscripts that focus on problems that are prevalent enough to affect a large proportion of the population (Dougherty et al., 2011). The interest in the articles that focus on common problems is based on the idea that more readers will tend to focus on common problems, so the journal will attract more readers. Editors also give priority to manuscripts that address the root causes of the problem. The researchers should therefore ensure during the design stage that the study is geared toward addressing the mystery of the mechanism of how the problem has evolved. Lastly, the editors are also concerned about whether the study addresses a problem that has broader societal implications.

The rigor of the research approach. The relevance of the manuscript and its suitability is also based on the research methods. For example, if the editors and reviewers ask whether the methods used are credible and sufficient enough to make the readers to adopt the research results with confidence and to apply them in another setting, the editors are concerned with both the adequacy of the research methodology in the research setting and its adequacy when applied to other settings. The aspects of the research methodology that the editors look for include whether the adopted methods result in findings that are generalizable to different settings and whether the adopted methodology has any influence on the work of future researchers and policymakers (Katz, 2009).

Determination of Relevance for Different Kinds of Studies

The relevance of the different studies varies based on the aim of such studies. For example, the relevance of studies that focus on cause and effect is based on the power of the causality. Thus, researchers who carry out cause-and-effect studies need to ensure that their studies demonstrate at least strong effects of innovation or otherwise show power to establish causality of the innovation (Katz, 2009).

For studies that deal with assessing processes, the determination of the relevance is based on the quality or value of the process or procedure itself. Therefore, researchers whose topics deal with the examination of a process need to ensure their findings provide an elaborate description of the performance of the examined process or the quality of the products obtained from the examined process. Thus, it is recommended that researchers need to understand and demonstrate how their research influences the readers or at least adds value to their work or way of thinking.

Originality and Topicality

Researchers need to ensure the manuscript meets the originality and topicality requirements. The originality and topicality of the manuscript are established by situating the arguments on authoritative research (Katz, 2009). Originality and topicality can also be demonstrated by referencing recent literature. For example, the researchers who situate their research question on the foundation that the problem of interest warrants investigation because it has not been investigated for several years need to anchor such arguments on recent research that shows new developments in data gathering techniques or evidence from indirectly related fields that demonstrate research into the problem is required (Dougherty et al., 2011). However, researchers should not fall into the trap of looking for recent literature at the expense of not using \ seminal research that may be important in anchoring the methodology and the theoretical framework.

Manuscript Relevance Checklist

Table 18 provides a summary of the major aspects of the manuscript that determine its relevance to the selected journal. Students need to ensure that their manuscript fulfills each of these aspects. The checklist provided in Table 18 may not be exhaustive because the different editors and journal may have varying relevance determination criteria; therefore, researchers should thoroughly assess the relevance criteria that are unique to the selected journal.

Table 17

The Summary of the Major Aspects of the Manuscript That Determine Its Relevance

Item	Description
Item 1	Is the research relevant to the focus of the journal or its audience?
	Does the manuscript address vital problems?
	Is the study worth doing?
	Do the quantitative studies have accepted a level of generalizability? Is the participant selection process transparent, and are the setting and intervention or materials well described?
	Do the qualitative studies offer theories that are generalizable or transferable to other contexts and people?

Avoiding Plagiarism

Plagiarism is the act of presenting other researchers' work without fully acknowledging them. In research, the work is considered plagiarized if it contains ideas, methods, or writings from others that have not been fully acknowledged (Wajdi, Sumartana, & Hudiananingsih, 2018). Plagiarism is, therefore, a form of copying or stealing other people's ideas. It should be noted that most plagiarism in academic writing and research is committed unintentionally or through reckless writing (Roig, 2006). Therefore, researchers need to understand the different forms of plagiarism to avoid committing such offenses.

Avoiding plagiarism should form the basis of writing quality manuscripts. Committing plagiarism in research constitutes a dishonest act and is therefore considered a breach of ethical principles, which can lead to the rejection of the manuscript (Roig, 2006). Plagiarized work can also have long-term effects on the researcher's career and should be avoided at all cost.

Forms of Plagiarism to Look Out For

Verbatim quotation without clear acknowledgment. This is where the author quotes the work of another researcher word for word without acknowledging them. Such quotations should be identified by the use of either quotation marks or indentation and with full referencing of the sources (Kumar, Priya, Musalaiah, & Nagasree, 2014). Citing the quotation varies based on the writing format. An example in APA format is like this: "Insert the text" (author, year of publication, page number).

Cut and paste from internet sources. Material that is obtained from internet sources needs to be acknowledged fully by indicating the author or the organization.

Paraphrasing. Paraphrasing is the most common form of plagiarism that is committed by students. This form of plagiarism is committed due to poor writing style or time pressure, or students do it intentionally. Paraphrasing can result in plagiarism if the writer adopts the same reporting structure or makes a limited alteration in a few words and the order of arguments without acknowledging the source (Roig, 2006). However, students need to note that acknowledging the sources of the paraphrased worked does not fully serve to exempt the writing from being classified as plagiarized. Thus, you should attempt to write a summary of the author's overall argument in your own words.

Inaccurate citations. This is a form of plagiarism that is often committed unintentionally by students, especially when using and acknowledging information obtained from a secondary source, not the primary source. Sometimes students write the entire article then go on a fishing expedition to look for articles to support their work, and they end up including articles and books in their references or bibliography they did not consult. Another form of plagiarism is auto-plagiarism, where an author fails to acknowledge the use of his or her previous work; another is the failure to acknowledge assistance that was received during the completion of the work such as the acknowledgment of the contribution of statisticians (Roig, 2006).

What Are the Consequences of Plagiarism?

In research, plagiarism has far-reaching consequences. Plagiarized articles can result in the withdrawal or the retraction of the article, cancellation of the article, and the replacement of the article (Wajdi et al., 2018). Authors who commit plagiarism may also face the additional punishment of being banned from sending articles to the affected journal.

Should Every Sentence Be Cited?

Not all sentences need to be cited. Some of the content in your article may constitute general common knowledge, which needs not be cited. General common knowledge varies across different fields, and the author with good mastery of the field should be able to distinguish general common knowledge from what is not (Kumar et al., 2014). Information that is considered to be in the public domain, such as the generally accepted dates of historical events such as World War I and II, is considered general common knowledge and therefore needs not be cited. Additionally, field-specific common knowledge also does not need to be cited. An example of field-specific common knowledge is the fact that salivary amylase that is produced in the mouth helps in the digestion of starch. However, the author needs to ensure that the field-specific common knowledge used and not cited is widely known within that field and understood as such by the target audience (Roig, 2006).

When to Paraphrase and When to Quote

The frequency of quoting or paraphrasing varies across different fields. For humanities papers, quoting is common, while summarizing is common in social or natural sciences. The use of quotes is often aimed at showing that an authority supports the point that you are putting across. Quotes are also used when one is trying to present a position or argument to critique (Kumar et al., 2014). The use of quotes in research papers also helps preserve the meaning of passages that can otherwise be lost if they are paraphrased or summarized. However, if the language used is not of much importance as the idea, authors are always encouraged to summarize the work of others and put the writing in their own words.

How Can I Avoid Plagiarism?

Students and novice researchers can avoid plagiarism through diligent writing. Various recommendations, such as those listed below, can be taken to minimize the occurrence of plagiarism in written articles (Kumar et al., 2014).

Understand the context. It is important to understand the ideas well enough to be able to restate them in your own words. Read and understand the passage as a whole.

Be selective. You need to identify what needs to be paraphrased or quoted. Only use the sections of written work that will help you make a point.

Read while taking notes. To ensure your article consists of your own words, spend time reading other researchers' work while writing down the main points to incorporate into your work. The written notes can then be used to develop arguments using your own words but acknowledging the source of the incorporated notes.

Changing the words and structure. Some texts can be hard to summarize without altering the meaning. In such scenarios, if the author does not want to quote the text, it is advisable to change the structure by starting at a different place in the passage. The author can also break up long sentences and combine short ones. The second step is to change the wording by using synonyms or a phrase that expresses the same meaning.

Manage your citations. It is important to maintain a record of sources while writing rather than searching for relevant source articles after completing the writing. The commonly used examples of software that help in the management of citations are EndNote and Reference Manager. Avoid referencing the literature review of a given article as the primary source of information, but instead reference the individual articles referred to in the review.

What Tools Can I Use to Check Plagiarism?

Commonly used tools to check plagiarism include Turnitin, Similarity Check, iThenticate software, PlagScan, and Plagiarism Checker.

Assessing the Quality of the Manuscript before Submission

Table 18 provides a summary of the points that should be considered when assessing the quality and readiness of the manuscript for submission

Table 18

Checklist for Assessing the Quality of the Manuscript

Section of Interest	Criteria
Title	Check if the title accurately reflects the paper content.
	Check if the significant words in the title are near the beginning.
Abstract	Check if the abstract adheres to the required number of words.
	Check if the abstract summarizes all the required paper sections, including the introduction, purpose, methods, results, discussion, and conclusion.
	Check if the selected keywords best allow the locating of the study.
Introduction	Check if the introduction begins with a broad issue related to the research area and narrows to the specific gap.

	Check if the relevant literature that is related to the research topic and that leads to the research gap is described in the introduction.
	Check if the introduction identifies the statement of the problem and the aim/hypothesis of the research.
	Check if it describes the originality of the research objectives by establishing the need for investigations in the topic area.
	Check if it gives a clear idea of the target readership.
	Check if it gives the originality and topicality of the manuscript.
	Check if the originality and topicality has been met by examining how the literature is used to anchor the research questions.
	Check if the information presented in the introduction naturally leads to the aim. You need to review the introduction if the explicit aims come as a surprise.
Methods	Check if the methods including statistical analysis appropriate for the questions addressed and the study.
	Check if there is clear and elaborate description of materials and methods in a manner that allows the determination of the credibility of the results.
	Check if the research is replicable.
	Check if the research is repeatable.
	Check if the research is robust.
	Check if the research has adhered to best practice.
Results	Check if the results provide answers to the questions raised in the introduction or address the study objectives.
	Check if the results are presented in a logical order in which the aims and the methodology are presented.
	Check if the tables and figures used in the manuscript are relevant and actually required. Could any be combined or deleted? Do they stand alone?
	Check if there is coherence in the description of results.
	Check if the findings are presented in the simplest

	possible terms.
	Check if the presentation of the findings makes reference to statistical analyses, such as significance or goodness of fit.
	Check if the results are plausible.
	Check if the observed trends support the paper's discussion and conclusions.
Discussion	Check if the original aim/hypothesis/question are mentioned in the beginning of the discussion.
	Check if the discussion has provided adequate comparison of the results and the relevant findings from the literature.
	Check if the discussion has provided adequate reasons or speculation regarding the observed similarities and differences between the results and the relevant findings from the literature.
	Check if the discussion provides adequate statements regarding the significance of the findings, inherent limitations, and implications for practice and/or future research directions.
	Check if the discussion evaluates the trends observed and explains the significance of the results to a wider understanding.
	Check if the discussion gathers all information into a single whole.
Conclusion	Check if the appropriate conclusion is based on the findings and discussion is provided.
	Check if the conclusion reflects upon the aims, and determine if they were achieved or not.
	Check if the conclusion is evidence-based.
References	Check if the references are complete and based on the required format.
	Check if the references adequately support the important parts of the argument.
	Check if the references are relevant.
	Check if the references are recent.
	Check if the references are readily retrievable.

CHAPTER 11: INTERACTION WITH THE EDITORS

Authors and editors constantly communicate during the period between the submission of the manuscript and the final decision on the publishing or the rejection of the manuscript. For researchers who are new to article publishing, communication with the editors can be daunting, especially when the submitted manuscript is heavily criticized. This chapter provides guidelines on how researchers should address communicating with the editor. The aspects that are addressed include the following:

- Responding to editors
- How to address the rejection of a manuscript

Responding to Editors

Given the time that the researcher has to spend writing the manuscript, it is sometimes challenging for them to accept critical comments about their work. However, for a successful publication of the manuscript, the researcher should be open to the fact that rarely is he or she always completely right or completely wrong (Cummings & Rivara, 2002). Similarly, the researcher should know that rarely is the referee or the editor always completely right or completely wrong. Therefore, when addressing the referees' or editor's comments, the researcher should strive to address the comments without compromising the message of the paper (Guyatt & Haynes, 2006). When addressing the editor's comments, it should not appear as though you are trying to demonstrate that you know it all; rather, you should demonstrate willingness to learn and improve the paper (Cummings & Rivara, 2002). In case the manuscript is rejected, you should consider other journals.

How to Address the Rejection of a Manuscript

It is disheartening when a manuscript is rejected, and it can cause anxiety and panic when you are under pressure to submit and publish within a limited period. Thus, it is important to adequately prepare, do quality writing, and choose the appropriate journal to avoid rejection (Day, 2011). However, despite ones' best efforts, a manuscript can be rejected for one reason or another. The rejection of the manuscript does not necessarily mean that the presented science is wrong. In fact, rejection is not uncommon. A short talk with established researchers will demonstrate that most of them have had their manuscripts rejected at some point in their careers (Peregrin,

2007). Discussing with someone in your discipline about rejection helps calm the nerves and allows one to focus on getting the work published (Peregrin, 2007).

The first step the researcher should take following the rejection of the manuscript is to establish the cause of the rejection. One of the reasons a manuscript can be rejected is that the content of the paper may not fit the scope of the journal (Chapman & Slade, 2015). The mismatch between the paper and the journal scope and aims can occur when the paper is too specialized or when its focus falls outside the focus of the journal (Chapman & Slade, 2015). Another reason that can lead to the rejection of a manuscript is the presence of clear and obvious flaws in the science. Further, poor language or structure can also result in the rejection of the manuscript by the editor (Ali, 2010). However, a manuscript can sometimes be rejected by high-ranking journals even if the reviews were (mostly) positive.

If the editor rejects the manuscript before submitting it to referees, revise it and submit it to a more appropriate journal. If the paper was submitted to referees, consider their comments, but remember that you need to preserve the storyline. If the manuscript was rejected but the editor's comments suggest you should revise and resubmit, then consider making the necessary revision without altering the main message (Ali, 2010).

Sometimes the rejection can occur as a result of the referees not understanding the paper enough to appreciate it. Rejection can also occur because of unclear recommendations from the referee to the editor. In such cases, one can appeal to the editor; however, exercise caution when appealing because there is a high chance of a negative response. The best option following rejection is to revise and submit to a new journal. However, if you choose to resubmit to the same journal, write a letter to the editor explaining the improvements made and why you think the paper should be reconsidered (Ali, 2010; Chapman & Slade, 2015).

Researchers should also consider duplicate and prior publications. A manuscript is considered a duplicate publication if its content overlaps substantially with an already published article that the author of the manuscript has not clearly and visibly referenced (International Committee of Medical Journal Editors, 2016). Prior publication, on the other hand, is a manuscript that contains information that has been released to the public domain.

Students need to ensure their manuscripts are original. However, for the already publicly available material, the writer needs to provide a clear acknowledgement of such. Without proper acknowledgment, the manuscript runs the risk of being rejected. Therefore, to avoid the misuse of resources (i.e., time and money) on manuscripts that would be rejected, authors need to ensure that their work is original. In addition, duplicate publications and submission of prior publications are violations of international copyright laws and ethical conduct, which should be avoided (International Committee of Medical Journal Editors, 2016).

To avoid conflict with the editor, referees, and the readership, the author needs to fully acknowledge the extensive use of already published material. The letter of submission submitted by the author alongside the manuscript should indicate that the manuscript has reported work that has already been reported in large part in a published article or has been submitted for publication elsewhere. It is also the responsibility of the author to provide the copies of the related material to the editor to help the editor and referees in handling the submission.

To this point, it is important to caution researchers on material that they choose to present in a scientific meeting. Although the presentation of part of the findings in scientific meetings in the form of posters or an abstract does not necessarily prevent the manuscript from being published, provision of extensive data can cause you problems during publishing. Thus, it is good practice to avoid presenting tables or figures that will be included in the manuscript. It is also important for researchers to consider how the dissemination of material that is presented in scientific meetings or conferences might affect the assigning of the priority to the manuscript by journal editors.

Researchers should take responsibility for the preprint versions of the work. The researchers need to inform the editor about the reprints and provide the copies of the preprint versions of the work to the editor. Once published, the authors need to amend the preprint versions to ensure the readers are directed to the final published article. It should be noted that sometimes a duplicate publication could be published without being identified by the editor. Such duplicate publication warrants retraction with or without the author's explanation or approval (International Committee of Medical Journal Editors, 2016).

In some cases, researchers may be faced with the dilemma of whether to immediately share with the public the results on critical issues that might result in saving lives or waiting until the work is published. The authors with such crucial data (e.g., public health emergency data) may want to release the data immediately but do not want to risk the manuscript being considered prior publication (International Committee of Medical Journal Editors, 2016). It is good practice to identify the journals that recognize and prioritize the best interest of public health. Such editors are likely to publish the manuscript even if the results had been made public.

CHAPTER 12: TIME SAVING TOOLS AND

STRATEGIES

Researchers should be good managers of time. They need to have good organizational skills, and they should plan well— and execute their plans to the letter. For students, writing and publishing research that is aimed at meeting certain academic requirements is a daunting job that requires good time management. The research intrigues along with other academic commitments may result in limited time for research if an effective way of managing the research work is not devised. Thus, this chapter provides suggestions and guidelines on how to best manage the research process to ensure effective use of the available time. The aspects that are discussed include these:

- Time planning strategies
- Time management tools used in research

Time Planning Strategies

Plan and Begin Early

You will best hone your research skills through practice and experience. Therefore, it is likely that your first research could be the longest because there will be starts and stops along the way.

You will need to read extensively to equip yourself with the knowledge that will help you troubleshoot possible problems and better develop your plan of action. One of the most common mistakes students make is the failure to invest adequate time in extensive reading. They simply immerse themselves into the research, only to encounter problems they would have easily avoided by developing their knowledge in the area of interest.

Set Realistic and Attainable Goals

For you to manage your time well, it is best to set goals that are measurable, realistic, and attainable using the available resources and within the available time. Developing intermediate and immediate activities that guide the attainment of long-term goals can help you set realistic goals. You should also assign measurable objectives to a structured time limit. Develop the habit of periodically reviewing the set goals to determine the achievement rates and the possible barriers to achievement. In academic research, students are encouraged to write progress reports that document what they have achieved and their plans for the future.

Optimize Realistic Planning

The process of optimizing realistic planning involves the fragmentation of tasks by creating to-do lists and checking off tasks as they are completed. Complex activities should also be broken down into manageable portions with defined deadlines. For example, when writing the manuscript, researchers are advised to spread out the writing process over a given timeline, where the completion of each section is assigned a specific time limit. It is also advisable for researchers to amass resources (i.e., knowledge, money and research tools) before starting the research. Always seek to automate the processes as much as possible.

Prioritize Your Research

Research activities often compete with other activities for the attention of the researcher. It is the responsibility of the researcher to acknowledge the primacy of his/her work. You should also complete the objective based on the order of priority. Researchers need to effectively schedule the research work during the time of the week that has the fewest interruptions. One should also schedule a research sabbatical, which is dedicated to the completion of the research tasks.

Manage the Potential Distractions

Develop a research environment that is free from external distractions. The development of a distraction-free research environment can include actions such as turning off visual (such as TV) and auditory interruptions (such as any type disruptive noise). It is also important to carry out an honest appraisal of the potential barriers that hinder the attainment of the set research objectives. Researchers should also strive for a balanced life: one should get sufficient rest and regular physical exercise. Researchers should also avoid the temptation of multitasking because it results in unwanted distractions and does not increase productivity. Whenever possible, the researcher should involve a team in the completion of the research task. The team can refer to the supervisors and the technical team that helps in the statistical analysis of the obtained data or the individuals.

Look Out for Time Drains

Researchers need to guard against procrastination, interruptions, and a lack of discipline, which constitutes a poor time management loop among researchers. Procrastination involves the postponing of a high-priority task in favor of low-priority activity. Procrastination, which manifests among researchers when they decide to attend to interruptions (low-priority activities), is caused by the lack of self-discipline. Novice and even established researchers who are not self-disciplined can fall into the trap of attending to interruptions, which is evident by the cessation of a goal-directed activity in favor of self-gratifying activities. Attending to interruptions lead to low productivity that is manifested by the inability to meet set targets or poor-quality products as a result of the last-minute rushes. Most novice researchers who procrastinate usually console themselves by suggesting that they work best under pressure and therefore gladly indulge themselves in low-priority activities. However, seasoned researchers know too well that high-quality research work and manuscripts require a lot of time. Research is usually a back-and-forth activity that requires researchers to regularly look back and improve on the previous steps as more and more knowledge is gained.

Some of the sources of interruptions that researchers need to guard against include email, phone calls, texts or instant messages, and visits from coworkers. For researchers to avoid procrastinating, interruptions, and the lack of discipline, they need to honestly monitor how they use their time and identify possible causes of procrastination. Researchers also need to prioritize their work and plan adequately. They can also delegate low-priority activities so they can focus more on the high priority activities.

Time Management Tools Used in Research

The tools that are presented in this section will help the researcher in the development of the research idea, referencing, and documentation of the important information during research. Table 19 provides a summary of the common tools along with the common use.

Table 19

Example of the Commonly Used Tools in Research

Tools	Links	Use
Evernote	https://evernote.com	Note taking, organizing, task lists, and archiving
OneNote	https://www.onenote.com/hrd	Information gathering and multiuser collaboration, notes sharing
CmapTools	https://cmap.ihmc.us/cmaptools/cmaptools-download/	Concept mapping software that allows the creation of graphical nodes representing concepts as well as the connection of the nodes using lines and linking words to form a network of interrelated propositions
Freeplane	https://sourceforge.net/projects/f	Creation of mind maps and electronic outlines

	reeplane/	
MindMeister	https://www.mindmeister.com	Online mind mapping application that facilitates the visualization, sharing, and presentation of thoughts via the cloud
Bookends	https://www.sonnysoftware.com	Management of bibliographies and references when writing essays and articles
EndNote	https://endnote.com	Management of bibliographies and references for writing essays and articles
Mendeley	https://www.mendeley.com/?interaction_required=true	A reference manager that facilitates the management and sharing of research papers and generation of bibliographies for published articles
RefWorks	https://refworks.proquest.com	Management of bibliographies and references when writing essays and articles
Dropbox	https://www.dropbox.com	File hosting service that reduces busywork within the workspace
Google Drive	https://www.google.com/drive/	File storage and synchronization
Grammarly	http://www.grammarly.com	Digital writing tool assisting writing grammatical correct articles; also helps in the detection of plagiarism
Publisher	https://products.office.com/en-us/publisher	Useful in the designing the layout of the research article

REFERENCES

Adom, D., Adu-Gyamfi, S., Agyekum, K., Ayarkwa, J.,

Dwumah, P., Abass, K., ... & Obeng-Denteh, W. (2016). Theoretical and conceptual framework: Mandatory ingredients of a quality research. *Journal of Education and Human Development*, *5*(3), 158–172.

Agee, J. (2009). Developing qualitative research questions: A reflective process. *International Journal of Qualitative Studies in Education*, *22*(4), 431–447.

Akintoye, A. (2015). Developing Theoretical and Conceptual Frameworks. Retrieved from Jedm.oauife.edu.ng>uploads>2017/03/07

Ali, J. (2010). Manuscript rejection: Causes and remedies. *Journal of Young Pharmacists*, *2*(1), 3.

Anderson, M., Solarin, I., Gerver, S., Elam, G., MacFarlane, E., Fenton, K., & Easterbrook, P. (2009). Research note: the LIVITY study: Research challenges and strategies for engaging with the black Caribbean community in a study of HIV infection. *International Journal of Social Research Methodology*, *12*(3), 197–209.

Baron, M. A. (2008). Guidelines for writing research proposals and dissertations. *Division of Educational*

Administration: University of South Dakota, 1–52.

Bavdekar, S. B. (2016). Formulating the right title for a research. *Journal of the Association of Physicians of India*, *64*, 53.

Bonevski, B., Randell, M., Paul, C., Chapman, K., Twyman, L., Bryant, J., ... & Hughes, C. (2014). Reaching the hard-to-reach: A systematic review of strategies for improving health and medical research with socially disadvantaged groups. *BMC Medical Research Methodology*, *14*(1), 42.

Brizay, U., Golob, L., Globerman, J., Gogolishvili, D., Bird, M., Rios-Ellis, B., ... & Heidari, S. (2015). Community-academic partnerships in HIV-related research: a systematic literature review of theory and practice. *Journal of the International AIDS Society*, *18*(1), 19354.

Caelli, K., Ray, L., & Mill, J. (2003). "Clear as mud": Toward greater clarity in generic qualitative research. *International Journal of Qualitative Methods*, *2*(2), 1–13.

Chapman, C., & Slade, T. (2015). Rejection of rejection: A novel approach to overcoming barriers to publication. *British Medical Journal, 351*, h6326.

Churchill, H., & Sanders, T. (2007). *Getting your PhD: A practical insider's guide*. Los Angeles: Sage.

Cone, J. D., & Foster, S. L. (1993). *Dissertations and theses from start to finish: Psychology and related fields*. Washington, DC: American Psychological Association.

Creswell, J. W., & Creswell, J. D. (2017). *Research design: Qualitative, quantitative, and mixed methods approaches*. Los Angeles: Sage publications.

Cronin, P., Ryan, F., & Coughlan, M. (2008). Undertaking a literature review: A step-by-step approach. *British Journal of Nursing, 17*(1), 38–43.

Cummings, P., & Rivara, F. P. (2002). Responding to reviewers' comments on submitted articles. *Archives of Pediatrics & Adolescent Medicine, 156*(2), 105–107.

Day, N. E. (2011). The silent majority: Manuscript rejection and its impact on scholars. *Academy of Management Learning & Education, 10*(4), 704–718.

Dickson-Swift, V., James, E. L., Kippen, S., & Liamputtong, P. (2007). Doing sensitive research: What challenges do qualitative researchers face? *Qualitative Research*, *7*(3), 327–353.

Dine, C. J., McGaghie, W. C., Bordage, G., & Shea, J. A. (2015). Problem statement, conceptual framework, and research question. *Review Criteria for Research Manuscripts*, *19-25*.

Dougherty, M. C., Freda, M. C., Kearney, M. H., Baggs, J. G., & Broome, M. (2011). Online survey of nursing journal peer reviewers: Indicators of quality in manuscripts. *Western Journal of Nursing Research*, *33*(4), 506–521.

Eakin, E. G., Bull, S. S., Riley, K., Reeves, M. M., Gutierrez, S., & McLaughlin, P. (2006). Recruitment and retention of Latinos in a primary care-based physical activity and diet trial: The Resources for Health study. *Health Education Research*, *22*(3), 361–371.

Evans, M. (2007). Recent research (2000–2006) into applied linguistics and language teaching with specific reference to L2 French. *Language Teaching*, *40*(3), 211-230.

Fah, T. S., & Aziz, A. F. A. (2006). How to present research data. *Malaysian Family Physician*, *1*(2–3), 82.

Flamez, B., Lenz, A. S., Balkin, R. S., & Smith, R. L. (2017). *A counselor's guide to the dissertation process: Where to start and how to finish.* Hoboken, NJ: John Wiley & Sons.

Flory, J., & Emanuel, E. (2004). Interventions to improve research participants' understanding in informed consent for research: A systematic review. *Journal of the American Medical Association; 292*(13), 1593–1601.

Fulton, S., & Krainovich-Miller, B. (2010). Gathering and appraising the literature. *Nursing research: Methods, critical appraisal and utilization,* 56-80.

García, J. A., Rodriguez-Sánchez, R., & Fdez-Valdivia, J. (2014). The selection of high-quality manuscripts. *Scientometrics, 98*(1), 299–313.

Grange, R. I. (1998). Saving time, effort and tears: A guide to presenting results. *British Journal of Urology, 81*(2), 335.

Guyatt, G. H., & Haynes, R. B. (2006). Preparing reports for publication and responding to reviewers' comments. *Journal of Clinical Epidemiology, 59*(9), 900.

Habibzadeh, F., & Yadollahie, M. (2010). Are shorter article titles more attractive for citations? A crosssectional study of 22 scientific journals. *Croatian Medical Journal, 51*(2), 165–170.

Hart, C. (2018). *Doing a literature review: Releasing the research imagination*. Los Angeles: Sage.

Hartley, J. (2012). Titles are the hardest thing: How can we make them more effective? *Impact of Social Sciences Blog*. Retrieved from http://eprints.lse.ac.uk/51997/1/blogs.lse.ac.uk-Titles_are_the_hardest_thing_How_can_we_make_them _more_effective.pdf

Hergenrather, K. C., Rhodes, S. D., Cowan, C. A., Bardhoshi, G., & Pula, S. (2009). Photovoice as community-based participatory research: A qualitative review. *American Journal of Health Behavior, 33*(6), 686–698.

Hing, N., Breen, H., & Gordon, A. (2010). Respecting cultural values: Conducting a gambling survey in an Australian Indigenous community. *Australian and New Zealand Journal of Public Health, 34*(6), 547–553.

Hoppitt, T., Shah, S., Bradburn, P., Gill, P., Calvert, M., Pall, H.,

... & Sackley, C. (2012). Reaching the "hard to reach":
Strategies to recruit black and minority ethnic service
users with rare long-term neurological
conditions. *International Journal of Social Research
Methodology*, *15*(6), 485–495.

Huston, P., & Choi, B. C. K. (2017). Scientific writing: A guide
to publishing scientific research in the health
sciences. *Canada Communicable Disease Report*, *43*(9),
169.

International Committee of Medical Journal Editors. (2016).
Recommendations for the conduct, reporting, editing,
and publication of scholarly work in medical journals.
Retrieved from
http://www.medicc.org/mediccreview/documents/ICMJ
E.PDF

Kalyanasundaram, M., Abraham, S. B., Ramachandran, D.,
Jayaseelan, V., Bazroy, J., Singh, Z., & Purty, A. J.
(2017). Effectiveness of mind mapping technique in
information retrieval among medical college students in
Puducherry: A pilot study. *Indian Journal of Community
Medicine*, *42*(1), 19–23.

Katz, M. J. (2009). *From research to manuscript: A guide to scientific writing.* Berlin: Springer Science & Business Media.

Kennedy-Clark, S. (2013). Research by design: Design-based research and the higher degree research student. *Journal of Learning Design, 6*(2), 26–32.

Keyzer, J. F., Melnikow, J., Kuppermann, M., Birch, S., Kuenneth, C., Nuovo, J., ... & Rooney, M. (2005). Recruitment strategies for minority participation: Challenges and cost lessons from the POWER interview. *Ethnicity & Disease, 15*(3), 395–406.

Kumar, M. J. (2013). Editorial Commentry: Making your research paper discoverable: Title plays the winning trick. *IETE Technical Review, 30*(5), 361–363.

Kumar, P. M., Priya, N. S., Musalaiah, S. V. V. S., & Nagasree, M. (2014). Knowing and avoiding plagiarism during scientific writing. *Annals of Medical and Health Sciences Research, 4*(3), 193–198.

Latham, J. (2017). Conceptual Framework. Retrieved from http://johnlatham.me/frameworks/research- methods-framework/conceptual-framework/

LoBiondo-Wood, G., & Haber, J. (2014). *Nursing research-e-book: methods and critical appraisal for evidence-based practice.* Elsevier Health Sciences.

McKercher, B., Law, R., Weber, K., Song, H., & Hsu, C. (2007). Why referees reject manuscripts. *Journal of Hospitality & Tourism Research, 31*(4), 455–470.

McMillan, B., Green, J. M., Woolridge, M. W., Dyson, L., Renfrew, M. J., & Clarke, G. P. (2009). Studying the infant feeding intentions of pregnant women experiencing material deprivation: Methodology of the Looking at Infant Feeding Today (LIFT) study. *Social Science & Medicine, 68*(5), 845–849.

Messuri, K. (2015). Clarity in medical writing. *The Southwest Respiratory and Critical Care Chronicles, 3*(12), 56–58.

Neale, J., & West, R. (2015). *Guidance for reporting qualitative manuscripts.* Retrieved from https://psycnet.apa.org/record/2015-11906-002

Okpala, P. (2018). Assessment of the influence of technology on the cost of healthcare service and patient's satisfaction. *International Journal of Healthcare Management, 11*(4), 351–355.

Oliver, M. (2011). *Editorial perspective: Writing qualitative manuscripts*. Retrieved from https://www.txca.org/images/tca/Documents/Journal/Journal.Winter%20Spring%202011.FINAL.pdf#page=9

Osanloo, A., & Grant, C. (2016). Understanding, selecting, and integrating a theoretical framework in dissertation research: Creating the blueprint for your "house". *Administrative issues journal: connecting education, practice, and research, 4*(2), 7.

Peregrin, T. (2007). How to cope with manuscript rejection. *Journal of the American Dietetic Association, 107*(2), 190–193.

Pierson, D. J. (2004). The top 10 reasons why manuscripts are not accepted for publication. *Respiratory care, 49*(10), 1246–1252.

Polit, D. F., & Beck, C. T. (2004). *Nursing research: Principles and methods*. Lippincott Williams & Wilkins.

Randolph, J. J. (2009). A guide to writing the dissertation literature review. *Practical assessment, research & evaluation, 14*(13), 1–13.

Ransohoff, D. F., & Lang, C. A. (1997). Clinical guideline: Part

II: Screening for colorectal cancer with the fecal occult

blood test: A background paper. *Annals of Internal*

Medicine, 126(10), 811–822.

Rezvani, A., Chang, A., Wiewiora, A., Ashkanasy, N. M.,

Jordan, P. J., & Zolin, R. (2016). Manager emotional

intelligence and project success: The mediating role of

job satisfaction and trust. *International Journal of*

Project Management, 34(7), 1112–1122.

Rimando, M., Brace, A. M., Namageyo-Funa, A., Parr, T. L.,

Sealy, D. A., Davis, T. L., ... & Christiana, R. W. (2015).

Data collection challenges and recommendations for

early career researchers. *The Qualitative Report, 20*(12),

2025–2036.

Roig, M. (2006). *Avoiding plagiarism, self-plagiarism, and other*

questionable writing practices: A guide to ethical

writing. Retrieved from https://bsc.ua.edu/wp-

content/uploads/2017/07/plagiarism-1.pdf

Ryan, L., Kofman, E., & Aaron, P. (2011). Insiders and

outsiders: Working with peer researchers in researching

Muslim communities. *International Journal of Social*

Research Methodology, 14(1), 49–60.

Saah, A. A., & Osei, C. K. (2010). A guideline for choosing a working title for a research project at the tertiary education level. *Journal Academica, 1*(1), 24–28.

Saleem, H. (2015). The impact of leadership styles on job satisfaction and mediating role of perceived organizational politics. *Procedia-Social and Behavioral Sciences, 172*, 563–569.

Shebl, F., Poppell, C. F., Zhan, M., Dwyer, D. M., Hopkins, A. B., Groves, C., ... & Steinberger, E. K. (2009). Measuring health behaviors and landline telephones: Potential coverage bias in a low-income, rural population. *Public Health Reports, 124*(4), 495–502.

Simon, M. K., & Goes, J. (2011). Developing a theoretical framework. *Seattle, WA: Dissertation Success, LLC.*

Staggers, N., & Blaz, J. W. (2013). Research on nursing handoffs for medical and surgical settings: An integrative review. *Journal of Advanced Nursing, 69*(2), 247–262.

Testa, J. (2009). The Thomson Reuters journal selection process. *Transnational Corporations Review, 1*(4), 59–66.

Wajdi, M., Sumartana, I. M., & Hudiananingsih, N. P. D. (2018). Avoiding plagiarism in writing a research paper. *Soshum: Jurnal Sosial dan Humaniora [Journal of Social Sciences and Humanities]*, *8*(1), 94–102.

Wentz, E. A. (2013). *How to design, write, and present a successful dissertation proposal*. Los Angeles: Sage Publications.

Young, M. (2002). *The technical writer's handbook: Writing with style and clarity.* , Sausalito, CA: University Science Books.

APPENDIX I:

LINKS TO IMPORTANT CRITICAL APPRAISAL

WORKSHEETS

1. Systematic Reviews Critical Appraisal Sheet: https://casp-uk.net/wp-content/uploads/2018/03/CASP-Systematic-Review-Checklist-2018_fillable-form.pdf

2. Diagnostics Critical Appraisal Sheet: https://casp-uk.net/wp-content/uploads/2018/03/CASP-Diagnostic-Checklist-2018_fillable_form.pdf

3. Randomized Controlled Trials (RCT) Critical Appraisal Sheet: https://casp-uk.net/wp-content/uploads/2018/03/CASP-Randomised-Controlled-Trial-Checklist-2018_fillable_form.pdf

4. Critical Appraisal of Qualitative Studies Sheet: https://casp-uk.net/wp-content/uploads/2018/03/CASP-Qualitative-Checklist-2018_fillable_form.pdf

APPENDIX II: PRISMA CHART

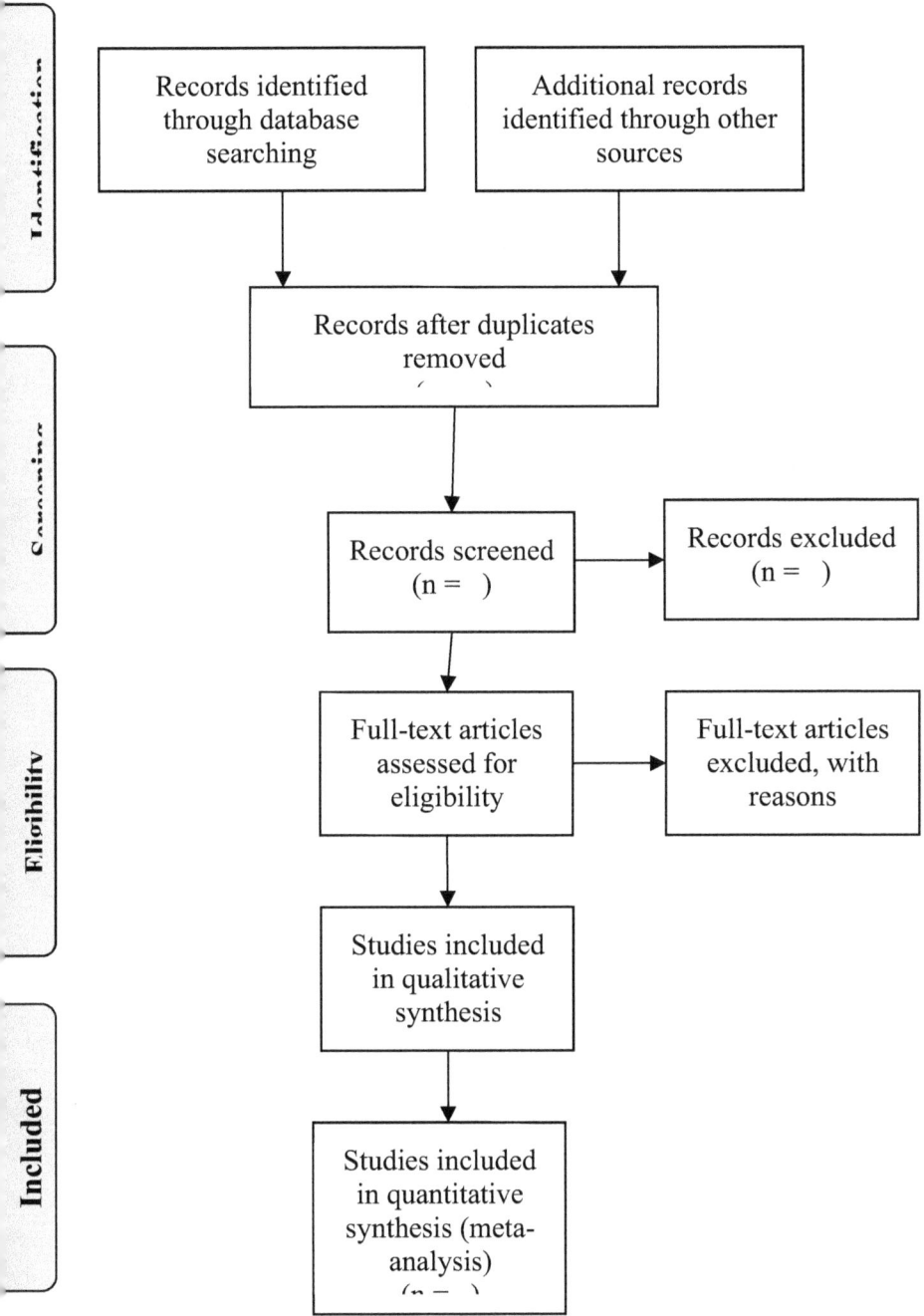

www.ingramcontent.com/pod-product-compliance
Lightning Source LLC
Chambersburg PA
CBHW072007090426
42740CB00011B/2131